Executive Video Interviews
in the
Hidden Job Market

Win C-Suite Jobs with Technical Brilliance and Authenticity

RAINER MARIA MORITA

Other books by Rainer Maria Morita:

Peak Performance Interviewing for Executives

Perfect Pitching for Executives in the Hidden Job Market

Executive Job Search in the Hidden Job Market - The Morita Method

Find Your Career Passion: Towards Abundant Joy, Fulfillment and Authenticity in Your Job, Career and Life

Globalization Opportunities for Executives in Japanese Companies

Tokyo Expat Job Search Guide

7 goldene Regeln für die erfolgreiche CEO-Stellensuche im verdeckten Stellenmarkt

Dedication

To win video interviews with ease, confidence, and authenticity.

Contents

PREFACE 1

INTRODUCTION 5

CHAPTER 1: YOUR GOAL 11

CHAPTER 2: SUCCESS IN THE HIDDEN JOB MARKET 17

VIDEO INTERVIEW SUCCESS

    CHAPTER 3: PILLAR 1: TECHNICAL CHOICES 47

    CHAPTER 4: PILLAR 2: YOUR HOLLYWOOD SETTING 83

    CHAPTER 5: PILLAR 3: YOUR INTERVIEW PERFORMANCE 107

CHAPTER 6: AUTHENTICITY 123

CHAPTER 7: PASSION 139

CONCLUSION 143

REFERENCES 145

APPENDIX 147

ABOUT THE AUTHOR 153

PREFACE

Since the COVID-19 pandemic changed life as we knew it in 2020, video interviewing has become the new de facto standard for companies everywhere. During the outbreak, hardly any significant organizations were conducting in-person interviews, and many firms sought quick ways to adjust their ways of working so they could keep up with the recruiting process. Despite the roll out of vaccines and resulting drop in COVID cases, video interviewing will still remain the new recruiting standard because of the many advantages it offers hiring firms, with the main advantage being time savings.

Video job interviews, compared to in-person interviews, save hiring managers 60% to 70% of time or even more in certain cases. While interviewers plan 60 to 90 minutes for a face-to-face interview, they put aside much less for video interviews.

Hence, the main challenge for interviewees is two-fold. On one hand, they have much less time as video interviews tend to be shorter with a more abrupt beginning and end. On the other hand, video technology reduces the impact interviewees can have on interviewers due to the virtual nature of the conversation, the limitations and challenges of technology, and the potential for distraction. Simply put, this book helps executives like you to rise and shine to peak performance in the video job interview despite these video technology challenges under higher time pressure.

In my role as International Hidden Job Market Expert and Executive Headhunter, I have been conducting about 700 video interviews annually over the last 10 years, and thus, I consider myself an extension of executives. Your success is my success. Your failure is my failure. In this book, I have gathered all my video interviewing know-how to show you what works and what doesn't.

My message is clear: Stop being an amateur.

Become a video interviewing pro.

This is not easy. It doesn't happen overnight. Success in video job interviews requires dedication, perseverance, and the willpower to transform yourself into the "YOU" brand that attracts employers enough for them to offer you the position.

THE THIRD BOOK IN THE TRILOGY OF INTERVIEW BOOKS

The third book *Executive Video Interviews in the Hidden Job Market* honors the meteoric ascent of video interviewing since the COVID-19 outbreak and places a strong emphasis on the technical aspects of mastering this digital media for interviews. This book not only teaches you how to prevent expensive blunders, but it also shows you how to maximize your performance during video interviews by setting up properly and acting accordingly.

As this is the third installation of this series, general interviewing practices and pitching practices are not the primary focus. Such methodological components are thoroughly covered in the previous two publications,

Peak Performance Interviewing for Executives and *Perfect Pitching for Executives in the Hidden Job Market.* But you can only use your full interviewing potential if you have a firm technical grasp of the video technology used for interviewing, which is what this book covers. Despite being self-contained, *Executive Video Interviews in the Hidden Job Market* is highly complementary to the previous two interview books, which the avid reader may choose to read.

Although video conferencing and video interviews are not new, most executives are disregarding, overlooking, or unaware of the shift in video technology becoming a mainstream recruitment norm. This book is therefore primarily a technical book which aims to fill that gap in the market and to give executives the technical and behavioural knowledge they need to succeed in video interviews in the Hidden Job Market.

INTRODUCTION

P rior to the pandemic, executives conducted video interviews via internet telephony applications such as Skype or WhatsApp from their mobiles. This brings to memory video telephony, which was used by many professionals to participate in real-time conversations from afar through small video display screens on their landline telephones. The fact, however, is this: despite the explosion of teleconferencing apps and platforms during the pandemic, many people are still not prepared to use these tools effectively in their day-to-day lives.

According to a survey conducted in February 2020 by Aptitude Research, an HR consulting firm, less than 60% of companies in the US used or planned to use video interviewing during their hiring processes prior to the pandemic, compared to 74% that adopted it two months later. After eight months, a survey collected by Gartner revealed that 89% of organizations were using video-based interviewing for recruitment.

In the first half of 2020, video platform service provider HireVue accounted for over 2 million virtual interviews. This number skyrocketed by the end of 2021, increasing to over 7.5 million. This indicates a whopping 275% increase in the number of interviews conducted over the platform. Companies which were unable to create platforms of their own relied on the existing and newly developed teleconferencing platforms to interview candidates for open positions such as Zoom, Microsoft Teams, GoTo-Meeting, Skype, Google Meet, ezTalks Meetings, StarLeaf, Cicso Webex, and a host of others.

Unfortunately, many executives were and are not aware of the impact of this shift and the challenges it poses to them. Even those who are a bit aware tend to consider video interviews as mere face-to-face interviews conducted over video. The reality, however, is that video interviews come with their own unique challenges which often have more to do with how to use the technology itself.

The implication of this, especially for jobseekers in a hiring process where all interviews except the last one tend to be video-based, is that you basically need to learn the skills of using the interview mode. Such professional and technical skills often include understanding how to use the technology and set it up, what the interviewers can see or shouldn't see, how to sit, your facial expression and gestures, and other tips which may impact your chances—both directly or indirectly.

This comprehensive guide equips you with video interview best practices and how to prepare for the process to impress interviewers. Remember, you are in for a competitive position—just like if you were auditioning for an acting role.

WHO IS THIS BOOK FOR?

This book is most relevant to executives and executive contenders undergoing a career transition. It also applies to all kinds of subject matter experts (e.g. legal, healthcare, tax, financial—just to mention a few).

This book is also useful for a broader audience: entrepreneurs who want to transition back into the corporate world; mothers returning to their careers after maternity leave; or those who had fallen sick and now have a desire to return to stable executive employment.

Additionally, anyone who conducts virtual meetings on a regular basis will find this reading to be helpful. Above all, there is a lot of room for development in many companies when it comes to those who sell and deliver in virtual settings. One example would be members of the digital salesforce who could perform better if they raised their digital selling skills.

I recall being interviewed about the craft of video interviewing while serving on a panel of experts for a globally televised event. After that incident, a US-based private equity partner who wasn't looking for work sent me a thank you email. I was interested in his motivation for joining and was thrilled to find that he wanted to increase his video proficiency for client acquisition.

Wow! I was impressed to hear that someone thought to practice his digital sales conversion abilities at a jobseeker event, especially since most jobseekers who could benefit from more practice with video interviews don't even think about it.

Finally, this book is not just for the technically savvy—in fact, it's quite the opposite. I assume that you, my reader, know a bare minimum about video, computers, and IT but not more. You are familiar with the internet, video capturing functions, and video calling without knowing the technical side of things. Oftentimes, others have probably set up your hardware devices for you to use in a plug-and-play fashion.

THE HUMBLE LEARNER

Before you start improving your interview skills in the digital world, you should adopt a curious mindset and a learning attitude while also possessing some humility. Most people ruin their own improvement efforts thinking they are already good, while the truth is they are probably good amateurs but not good enough in terms of their own professional interview performance. Saying to yourself, "I do not know what I do not know," is conducive to producing the best results.

I want to see you exploring what is best for you rather than assuming you have everything lined up already. Most of my clients are always taken by surprise when I point out to them the shortcomings in their digital way of interviewing.

The best comparison to illustrate your need for learning is when you are trying to take a professional headshot photo of yourself for job search purposes. You have seen on LinkedIn or elsewhere so many poor photos that make you laugh. That is why I always recommend my clients to go to a professional photographer. He has the process know-how, equipment, and experience to deliver an impressive photo. Doing it on your own means you are possibly making a fool of yourself and will only find out about it when others tell you that something is seriously wrong with your photo.

GOOD IS NO LONGER GOOD ENOUGH

You will hear this repeatedly throughout this book:

> **Good is no longer good enough.**

I see many jobseekers start their video interview with pre-corona era hardware which is already a compromise because the new normal computers are much more powerful machines. Guess what they are specifically designed for? Video communications.

Your goal in any job interview is similar to that of a Hollywood actor auditioning for a role. Be the best at whatever you are interviewed for. Similarly, the Hollywood actor aims at being the best actor. If you are best at interviewing, your chances of a job offer increase in your favor. The same goes for the actor—their chances of an Oscar nomination rise when they are the best actor.

So, why would anyone settle for an interview appearance that makes them appear like everyone else, like one of many? If you settle for mediocre interview standards and do not dare to challenge them, then you risk being perceived as mediocre.

Why did you buy this book and bother reading it? To stand out. So, with that being said, let's roll up our sleeves and get to work. And remember: good is no longer good enough. But after reading this book and applying these learnings, you are going to be great.

CHAPTER 1: YOUR GOAL

"Don't let the entire staircase overwhelm you. Just focus on the first step, and then the next one."
—Rainer Maria Morita

Your objective in video job interviews is to advance to the next step in the hiring process. That's it.

Getting an offer shouldn't be your first priority. As you are probably already aware, there are typically three to six interviews and numerous stakeholders involved in the hiring process for executives. In a one-meeting-to-offer process, it is quite unlikely that you would be able to convince everyone to come meet you and accept the terms of your employment. It's uncommon to receive an offer after the first or second round of interviews.

So, why would you attempt to receive an offer at the start of the process when you are already aware that it is highly unlikely to occur? You see that it is illogical. Instead, focus on taking one step at a time. Getting a lot of "yeses" quickly is the goal of job seeking. A step might be as simple as committing to provide the interviewer your compensation information in an Excel file. Never lose sight of the reality that this somewhat protracted process could end with an offer, but this offer is contingent upon receiving a "yes" at each interview gateway.

> *"Your goal in video job interviews is not to get an offer but to move to the next stage."* –Rainer Maria Morita

Always focus on what's next. Getting there is your goal.

SUCCESS FACTORS

Now that you understand your goal, let's talk about how to make this happen. First, you need some **success factors** to be in place for success with video interviews in the Hidden Job Market. These include:

- An entrepreneurial, proactive spirit of "Attitude Defines Your Altitude" with which you will be combing the market for the right executive opportunities
- Technical preparation for video technology to minimize risks and unwanted "surprises" including an impeccable video interview setting to impress your audience
- A bio and meeting documents to run video interviews efficiently
- A set of behaviour and pitching skills that will set you apart from others and assure maximum impact
- Authenticity and passion

A quick preview at this stage makes sense. I call such an executive who embraces these success factors to move his Hidden Job Market agenda forward with tenacity, relentless determination, and entrepreneurial drive the **"Morita Method Executive."**

The **"Morita Method Executive"** is someone who seeks or creates hidden career opportunities at the executive-level. The naming is based on my executive job search success system called "**The Morita Method**" for finding multiple six-figure executive opportunities in the Hidden Job Market.

SHIT HAPPENS

Before I show you how to interview successfully, I want to show what can possibly—and often does—go wrong in a video interview.

Technical preparation and minimizing risks were mentioned above in the success factors, but I'd like to talk a little more about them here as I think these are some of the most important yet too often neglected aspects of video interviewing.

Shit happens which we think could never happen in a million years. Can you believe that there was a recent board meeting on Zoom where the chairlady's mother walked out in the background completely naked? Yep, shit happens.

So, let's make sure it does not happen to you when you want it least: during your video interview.

Let me walk you through one disaster-type video interview with sound issues using Zoom. I call it "Case: Shit Happens."

———————— CASE: Shit Happens ————————

It is December 8, 2022 at 9am (Zurich local time), and you are on your third meeting to interview for a hidden job with a major company. You join the video interview 3-5 minutes before the agreed upon time and wait for the interviewer to let you in.

Once he joins at the top of the hour, you are automatically transferred from the waiting room into the virtual meeting room, and Zoom displays a short message saying: "Connecting to audio."

You see the interviewer, and he sees you—the long awaited moment is here. You both exchange greetings, perhaps accompanied by nice gestures and smiles.

The interviewer says, "Hello, nice to meet you. How are you?"

You smile and offer a similar greeting, only to be met by an unhappy, disappointed expression on the other side. He shakes his head to indicate "no, things do not work" and shrugs his shoulders.

"Connecting to audio" did not work for whatever reason. What happens now is what I call the "monkey scene."

You repeat, "Hello, can you hear me?" several more times and make monkey gestures to indicate you don't know what is going on.

The next phase makes the interviewer even more uncomfortable. Your monkey gestures become wilder and are accompanied by increasing levels of helplessness as you struggle to make your voice heard. You need to troubleshoot and quickly resolve the issue, while he is forced to just sit there and watch, expecting you to "work it out somehow."

We do not want to go into technical details here. It suffices to say that often headphones, especially the trendy bluetooth connected earphones are not automatically "connecting to audio."

Maybe the interviewee is a CFO or CEO who is not technology savvy and recently got a new laptop. Who knows?

Anyhow, by now five minutes have passed. Let us assume the interviewee is using earphones.

You are trying hard to make the earphones work. You continue changing your settings, both on Zoom and your computer. Repeatedly, you are asking: "Can you hear me?" but to no avail.

Finally, you pull out the earphones, switch audio back to your computer microphones, and reach a breakthrough. You hear the interviewer's voice. It seems too nice to believe. All of a sudden, you both can hear each other. You smile. The interviewer smiles back.

Oh my god. How annoying. By now, 10 minutes have passed. You only scheduled 30 minutes time. The interviewer looks at his watch as well, understands that maybe 15 minutes are left to talk with five minutes to wrap up, and feels the pressure already.

He suggests postponing the meeting, although it will be no earlier than in one month. You are extremely disappointed, but you agree, feeling as if there isn't really another option.

As your rescheduled interview date approaches, you get an email from the hiring manager thanking you for your time but also apologizing—the position has been filled and thus your upcoming interview is canceled. They say they'll reach out if anything similar opens up. They don't.

So, as you can see from this example, technical preparation and minimizing risks are crucial aspects of video interviews. Even the slightest hiccup, like not being able to connect to audio, can drastically reduce your chances of getting a job offer.

You'll never be able to advance to the next step in the interviewing process if you can't get past the one you are currently on.

CHAPTER 2: SUCCESS IN THE HIDDEN JOB MARKET

"Fish where the fish are."
—Old saying

B efore we dive into the "Morita Method Executive," we need to discuss the differences between Open and Hidden Job Markets.

An **Open Job Market interview** is an interview for a published job opportunity. The hiring company releases its job in printed or online media and invites jobseekers who apply in response to that advertisement, be it the corporate website or external advertising media. The Open Job Market interview is between a job applicant or jobseeker and a corporate decisionmaker.

A **Hidden Job Market interview** is a business discussion that centers on a business proposal made by an external executive in the hope of finding or creating a business case justifying his/her hiring. The Hidden Job Market executive is the initiator. He or she is initially in stealth mode and then switches the coin to career opportunity interviews to create demand for his or her hiring.

TERMINOLOGY MATTERS: THE MORITA METHOD EXECUTIVE

I call the Open Job Market interviewee a jobseeker or job applicant. I call the Hidden Job Market interviewee a "Morita Method Executive." While we've all been a jobseeker or applicant at one point, you might not be entirely clear on what a "Morita Method Executive" is. Let's talk about it.

Instead of attending open job interviews like jobseekers, the "Morita Method Executive" is someone who seeks or creates hidden, executive-level career opportunities and holds business meetings.

And no, this term isn't some deviously crafty way to promote my other books.

The main reason for the use of the term "Morita Method Executive" is that I want to strictly separate job applicants and jobseekers in the Open Job Market from those who create demand for themselves in the Hidden Job Market by building relationships with companies and decisionmakers interested in hiring them.

Using a metaphor, interviewing in the Open Job Market is like going to an actor audition. You are given a brief. The hiring organization has defined the interview process, and you must perform the best you can based on these specifications.

OPEN JOB MARKET INTERVIEWS

Before we turn our attention to the more obscure Hidden Job Market, let us make clear what video interviews in the Open Job Market look like these days.

If I am being utterly honest, most executives only have a faint idea of how much organizational effort is required to set up a video interview.

One assistant is usually tasked with setting up and coordinating such interviews. Typically, this is a recruiting coordinator, recruiting assistant, or, if such an assistant is lacking, recruiting manager/executive recruiter. Otherwise, the executive assistant or secretary of decisionmakers may also handle such tasks

Open job video interviews require:

- Schedule management of multiple parties—sometimes across multiple time zones
- Setting up and sharing the video solution invitation link
- Explanations of how to use such video solution
- Marketing collateral, if desirable, to share with the interviewee such as company brochure, explanation videos, etc.
- A professionally written and formatted video interview invitation email template—sample below:

Hello First Name,

This is the Talent Acquisition Team from Hiring Company ABC.

Thanks for submitting your availability for the Executive Position (location: Germany).

The interview will be processed online via

Microsoft Teams.

I have attached a PDF file to help you access MS teams. We recommend candidates to take a look at the instructions for setting up MS Teams before the scheduled interview date.

You're confirmed for your interview on:

- Date/Time: Apr 20, 2023 8:00am-9:00am CEST
- Interviewers: Head of Sales Engineering, HRBP, VP of BD
- Microsoft Teams LINK: https://teams.micro soft.com/1/meetup-join/19%3...

To add this interview appointment to your calendar, click HERE.

Please test the application before the interview to ensure a smooth interview process and join the link 15 minutes before schedule to test audio/video connection.

- Reference LINK (YouTube)
- All about Hiring Company (YouTube LINK)
- Job specification (PDF file)

In a nutshell, open job video interviews are the result of hard work and organizational discipline in getting systems and processes in place which ultimately requires someone tasked with managing this complex and time-consuming process. Nothing happens by chance.

Leaving it to chance or handling it spontaneously may occur in rare cases and is usually the source of many forms of video job interview troubles. To avoid these issues, companies typically systemize and organize their recruiting department.

From this information alone, we have already learned that even in the Open Job Market, companies need to spend a lot of time and money to organize and effectively run video job interviews.

Here is another important learning point. In an Open Job Market interview, the hiring company runs the show and does not like changes.

The hiring company's HR team is taking 100% control of the video interview process. They run the show, so to speak. The hiring manager is an add-on to this system. So, you can see how this precise, clockwork-like video interview process can quickly become dysfunctional if and when someone wants to make changes.

HIDDEN JOB MARKET INTERVIEWS

In Hidden Job Market interviews, you are like the film director and main actor at the same time. You have a story to tell, and as the film director, you think about how to create an awesome movie out of that story.

In the interview, you show up as the main actor of your own movie. As film director and main actor, you have the freedom to choose the "how."

I call this peculiar aspect of Hidden Job Market video

interviews "orchestrating a winning performance." Orchestrating a winning performance means you are responsible for all aspects of the video interview—yes, all of them.

Orchestrating a winning performance means you have the chance to turn every interview opportunity into a brand-representative, profitable performance.

The main difference between the Hidden Job Market video interview and Open Job Market ones are as follows:

Unique Aspects of Hidden Job Market Video Interviews:

1. The entrepreneurial attitude of the executive interviewee
2. Command of a process that is proactive, risk-containing, and ideally surprise-free
3. Different job search tools at different stages of the process
4. Storytelling via video
5. Video presentation skills

Let's discuss in detail each point and how it benefits you as a professional.

1. THE ENTREPRENEURIAL ATTITUDE OF THE EXECUTIVE INTERVIEWEE

As I explained in my book *Executive Job Search in the Hidden Job Market - The Morita Method*, searching for executive-level jobs in the Hidden Job Market is based on a new set of entrepreneurial rules. To find your perfect job, you must first understand these new job search rules, which I call "new job search economics." To become a successful player in the Hidden Job Market, it all starts with learning the system that governs job search success.

According to new job search economics, anyone in the labor market is a business.

Think of yourself as a business (Me Inc.). Andy Grove, ex-CEO of Intel Corporation, once said, "No matter where you work, you are not an employee. You are in business with one employer—yourself. Nobody owes you a career—you own it as a sole proprietor."

Manage yourself like a business. Even employees of a company should consider themselves self-employed individuals managing their Me Inc. business. Start thinking, acting, and job searching as a Me Inc. entrepreneur from this moment forward. Fill in your first and last name below—let's create your business now.

I am _____ Corporation.

ATTITUDE PROPELS YOUR ALTITUDE
Develop this entrepreneurial attitude and make yourself owner of your career.

The right entrepreneurial attitude for the MORITA METHOD is:

- I only select companies I want to work for.
- I only select companies in line with my Value Proposition and Growth Agenda.
- I only select companies where I can have my perfect job.
- I only select companies willing to pay what I am worth based on value and performance.

A Tesla executive client of mine, with whom I shared the manuscript of this book, commented on the importance of attitude in the following way:

"The most valuable takeaway for me is related to my attitude toward work. It was a pleasant surprise and a relief to see in writing what I've been thinking for years - that I am a service provider for the company and the business on its own, whether I am on a contract or freelance basis. I offer certain services, and in return, the company pays me for them. Therefore, a job interview is not just a one-way street where I answer questions - in fact, I am providing value to the company by taking on responsibilities for their business or part of their business. Rainer Morita's suggestion of negotiating my next position with this approach was a great reassurance that my perspective is valid. This realization didn't change my world, but it put me in a position where I should have been all along."

Such an attitude is proactive. Instead of waiting for certain positions to open up, you initiate direct contact with decisionmakers at the companies you selected.

This attitude is also contagious. It will shine through in interviews with executives, board members, and other stakeholders.

Most importantly, this attitude will lead to you landing multiple job offers in 120 days.

THE NEW JOB SEARCH ECONOMICS

In the new job search economics, you are not searching for a job. Rather, you are an investment that you are selling to a company. Therefore, target the companies and decision-makers most likely to hire you and discover opportunities invisible to you beforehand.

In the new job search economics, executive jobs are investment projects or joint ventures for your Me Inc. I see little difference between your job search and a private equity company investing in companies. Acquire, manage, and diversify your investment projects as you would with joint ventures.

The new job search economics is about creating business opportunities, not about looking for jobs. Be a business opportunity creator, not a jobseeker. Your job is to use your marketing skills to define your perfect job and plan a sales campaign that presents your best value to potential buyers. Like companies invest in marketing and sales, you, as owner of Me Inc., should invest in marketing yourself and selling your brand.

> **In the new job search economics, value is king.**

Your hiring does not depend on your skills or experience but rather on the value you will generate. Therefore, you must communicate value to the decisionmaker. You are recruiting a client, not a job. Therefore, understand the client's business problems and determine how you can help solve them. Only then can you show how much value your skills and experience will generate.

Value is the language you need to learn and master to succeed in the Hidden Job Market.

In the new job search economics, you market yourself as a unique and comprehensive solution provider. People who do not market themselves and their unique skillset become a common commodity. Common commodities sell at a low price or do not sell at all, which in this case means unemployment. What you can do well is going to be your best guarantor to creating extraordinary value.

In the new job search economics, the bar for success has been raised. Employers expect massive value as enticement to invest in your business. Competitors are equipping themselves with the best job search coaches, strategic advisors, mentors, and communication experts. Today, you must perform at a higher level than you performed yesterday, and even still, you must assure stakeholders that tomorrow's results will be better than today's.

The new job search economics is about becoming a person in demand and ensuring job security for a lifetime.

But don't beat yourself up about it. The first sale is to yourself. Be totally convinced that you have what it takes to succeed. Tell yourself you can do it from the start. The rest is only execution—and believe it or not, that's the easier part.

2. COMMAND OF A PROCESS THAT IS PROACTIVE, RISK-CONTAINING, AND IDEALLY SURPRISE-FREE

As a Morita Method Executive, I want you to stop thinking about job interviews as "interviews." Instead, think of interviews as business meetings.

In the Hidden Job Market, you want to have business meetings leading to business discussions during which you present and discuss your Unique Value Proposition. Therefore, you should forget about the term "interviews" and get excited about how to deliver a winning performance in your next video business meeting. Remember, turn every interview opportunity into a brand-representative, profitable performance.

Although the company you are speaking with technically has power and control over money and hiring, it is fair to say that you are playing the role of the interviewer. In your business discussion, you guide the conversation. Start strong with your Unique Value Proposition, ask probing questions, ask for clarification, deep dive into important matters, then bring the conversation to an end when you feel the timing is right. You play a leading role—not your counterpart.

I always observe the rather negative influence of the words "interview" and "interviewer" on executives. It's interesting because if you tell executives they are going to a business meeting, there is no change of behaviour. They remain natural.

But if you tell executives about an upcoming interview, then they immediately start showing signs of nervousness. They start to think of themselves as 10 times smaller than they really are and look up to the interviewer as some kind of god. They become unnatural and oftentimes victims of adrenaline, which can have devastating consequences for their interview success.

You should remove such limiting thoughts about interviews and interviewers in the traditional sense from your mind.

There are, however, scenarios where your counterpart is playing a dominant role during the meeting, and in such cases, the interviewee-interviewer relationship in the traditional sense holds true.

In order to not confuse you, though, I will keep using the terms interviewee and interviewer in this book. But in the back of your mind, remember that you are a driving and unifying force in Hidden Job Market conversations.

COMMANDING THE PROCESS

So, how do you command the process in this business-meeting-style interview?

First and foremost, you decide the medium for the interview as well as the perceived topic of discussion.

Executives like the convenience of emails. I mean, don't we all?

Emails do, however, require you to give up control over communication. The ability to reach out to the decisionmaker by telephone is a matter of control. Calling is the fastest way to reach them, and you have their full attention whilst speaking with them over the phone. You can fix an appointment, suggest the topic of the call, and notify him or her of any meeting collateral you plan to send. For this reason, pick up the phone.

And while you are probably leaning towards calling your meeting an "interview" (because in your mind, that's what it is), you might be surprised to learn about **the incredible power of just having a "chat."**

I had a job seeking, commercial leader type executive client in central Africa with 15 years of successful track record in a well-known power tools company called Atlas-Copco. He had accepted a well-paid job in the mining industry in Africa—an unknown player in the industry. He and his family decided after one year that they missed European culture and lifestyle, so they decided it was time to relocate to Europe. To his surprise, no headhunter or company wanted to interview him. That is when he engaged me.

As a previous regional sales director, he had a broad and strong network including CEOs and chairmen of well-known publicly listed companies, which is fantastic from a Hidden Job Market perspective. But, to his disappointment, week after week, there were no interviews.

"Really? Really no interviews at all?" I asked.

"None," he confessed. "But…"

He then explained to me that he had chats with one of his ex-colleagues who became chairman of a big, famous German company. The week after he told me this, he had another chat with a colleague who had become CEO of a worldwide market-leading Swiss company. In both cases, it was just a short 10 to 15 minute call to "catch-up" and ask them for introductions to other companies.

Eventually, one of these "chats" led to another "chat" with a top executive from a company that ended up hiring him.

Chats with direct trusted contacts are worth gold. Such calls are necessary precursors to Hidden Job Market interviews that materialize because you have casual chats with very well-connected top executives who act as door openers or springboards for your Hidden Job Market job search. Every business meeting is an opportunity to add value to the relationship or to pitch the interviewer on your vision and agenda.

> The 4 words to avoid in your communication
> for meeting set up and the pursuit of invisible jobs are:
>
> ## 1. Interview
> ## 2. Interviewee
> ## 3. Interviewer
> ## 4. Resume

But, if he had asked these executives for an "interview," he might not have gotten that far. Why? Because if they don't have positions to fill, then they aren't going to take the time to schedule interviews. Therefore, labeling the meeting as an "interview" may do more harm than good to your Hidden Job Market search and close doors which were otherwise available.

For that very reason, you should also avoid using the words "interviewee," "interviewer," and "resume." Think about it like being in stealth mode—you're simply suggesting and running business meetings, not insinuating an interview.

Interviews and resumes are Open Job Market tools used for applying for open jobs. With the mention of words like "interview" and "resume," you force the question that can easily terminate all your efforts to progress in the Hidden Job Market:

"This person (i.e., you) sent a resume, but for what role? We don't have a role at the moment. I'll have HR send him a rejection note."

You force the party receiving your resume to conclude that your application should be rejected because there is no job for you at the moment. In other words, the resume closes all doors.

Using any of those four words is equal to putting your foot in the mouth because:

1. The resume is a formal document, but at the early stages of exploring opportunities, you cannot

    point your resume at a specific opportunity—it is pointless

2. The resume should be stored in the company's candidate database, making it more difficult to hide that interviews are going on from HR
3. By making this a "formal" interview process, you're making things complicated for the executive by:
   a. Forcing them to abide by HR rules and guidelines
   b. Making them feel like they are overstepping others in their company who typically run interviews
   c. Posing as a risk to internal C-suite candidates

However, I am not saying you should never use those words. At some stage of the process, people may ask for your resume. When decisionmakers ask for your resumes or ask that you send it to a certain contact of yours, try—according to your judgement of assessing the whole situation—to suggest sending your executive biography, a short PowerPoint presentation, or something in video format.

The resume is the document that nobody likes. The resume does not sell you and can cause you all kinds of problems. Try to avoid sending it by offering other documents that do a much better job at furthering your cause. Only as a last resort should you send your resume during the early stages of Hidden Market interviews.

When you are at or almost at the offer making stage, companies may need a legal document. In big companies, C-suite hiring is subject to formal assessments such as the hiring committee reviewing your case. That is when a resume is, or may be, needed.

THE POWER OF DISTRACTION

Since you are now in command of the "interview," it is your responsibility to capture the interviewer's attention and keep them focused.

Achieving focus in a distracted world is a challenge of its own.

The level of distraction that affects the interviewer during in-person and digital interviews varies significantly; however, I dare say that nowadays moderate to severe distraction during the digital interview is the norm.

Everything that prevents the interviewer from focusing on your interview is considered a distraction. Distraction can take a variety of forms, including:

- Ringing on a mobile or landline phone
- Email notification of a new message
- Push alerts for computer apps
- Animals/insects approaching the interviewer or making sounds
- People entering the room, approaching the interviewer, or creating noise
- A postman delivering packages
- Loud noises outside—anything from fireworks and

sirens to lawnmowers and chainsaws
- Community announcements
- Nearby lighting changes

I see distraction as a major risk to your interview success as the interviewer may not catch all the details of what you are sharing, causing them to miss valuable insights. And unfortunately, you may not be able to spot distractions nor prevent them.

Luckily, there are a few things you can do to help reduce the likelihood of your interviewer becoming distracted.

First, try to magnetize the interviewer to you.

You must pay great attention to and actively participate in your interview. Bring him or her to focus on you, which you can do by being more animated, interactive, and physically active than you would be in a face-to-face interview.

Think about yourself as a TV show moderator or talkmaster, not a news anchor. For example, talkmaster Larry King with his show Larry King Live understood that his audience wanted to be both educated and entertained.

Ask your interviewer questions that require his attention or a response. Ask them if they need a break if you sense that they are being distracted (for instance, if they are glancing to the left, right, or under the desk because a pet is rushing around).

And finally, keep your responses short—ideally two minutes or less. When you ramble on in your answers to interview questions, the interviewer quickly gets bored and loses interest. Lengthy answers can also become convoluted, while shorter responses tend to be clearer and more direct, making it easier for the interviewer to understand and take note of your key points.

Keeping your interviewer focused on you will help ensure they aren't missing any piece of your Unique Value Proposition.

HOW TO MAKE VIDEO JOB INTERVIEWS SURPRISE-FREE

Now that you understand the importance of being proactive and commanding the process, let's talk about how to keep your interviews surprise-free by mitigating risk. Because what good is commanding the process if you cannot prevent, or at least reduce, unwanted surprises and other risks?

Executives are usually armed to the teeth in business with regards to risk prevention, risk management, and risk mitigation, but they are too often amazingly unprepared in video job interviews when things go astray.

You must prepare for the scenario of video job interviews possibly going wrong because minor things can ruin your show and obliterate any opportunity you otherwise could have brought to a winning end. In the Hidden Job Market, you need to be more proactive to think ahead of what possibly could go wrong and have quick emergency support available.

In the Open Job Market, the hiring company often prepares

you for the interview, but in the Hidden Job Market, you need to include the interviewer in your preparation and be ready to jump in with quick, effective troubleshooting. This is because success for you only happens if you both perform well and enjoy the video interview. If anything goes wrong, it risks ruining the movie.

Therefore, I want you to understand this: you should be able to assure a smooth video interview by making the process as smooth and efficient as possible for both parties.

It also means it is upon you to investigate possible ways to troubleshoot failures and defects on the interviewer's side and have ideas, suggestions, and tricks to quickly overcome minor glitches, problems, or failures to "continue your movie."

In the Open Job Market, inhouse executives and corporate recruiting departments often have recruiting assistants or secretaries for a simple reason: to take care of all those little details in the set up and management of the video interview to assure its success.

In the Hidden Job Market, it is different. You are in charge. It is your movie, and the interviewer or decisionmaker is part of your movie. You better make sure he or she is able to perform as you want and need them to in order for everyone to feel good about the experience and be successful.

You are a hidden troubleshooter and emergency support in case things go wrong. You need to think in advance, jump in, and support them as needed if things do not go as expected.

3. DIFFERENT JOB SEARCH TOOLS AT DIFFERENT STAGES OF THE PROCESS

In the Open Job Market, it all starts with your resume and possibly also a cover letter. But in the Hidden Job Market, as we've discussed, the resume comes later in the process or at the end of the process. Exceptions are possible, depending on the type of company and decisionmaker.

While you might not need a resume right away in the Hidden Job Market, you will need a bio and simple tools for meeting set up, notes, and follow up, as well as solid visualization and presentation documents.

SETTING UP A MEETING CORRECTLY WITH BIOS AND AGENDA ITEMS

Do you know the feeling of consenting to meetings without having any prior knowledge about your counterpart or what specifically they want to talk about?

> **Before a Hidden Job Market interview, clarify the WHO and the WHAT—WHO you are and WHAT you want to talk about.**

Having an executive biography ready and preparing talking points can be the difference between making a great impression and not making one at all.

An executive biography, or "bio," is a short story about an executive's career and background. In the past, mainly artists, writers, and politicians have used bios. With the advent of social media, every executive faces a more transparent "always on" world that wants to know about them. Usually, interviewers briefly investigate your LinkedIn profile summary and professional experience. However, you are dealing with busy decisionmakers who probably don't even know this is an interview at all. So, don't expect them to check out your LinkedIn profile beforehand.

This is also why every executive increasingly benefits from the use of his/her own bio, which is a one- to two-page biography in PDF format with a nice headshot. The bio captures the executive's career milestones, achievements, distinguishing features as a leader, and other noteworthy aspects such as philanthropy, affiliations, professional memberships, and perhaps family information.

In addition to your bio, the topic of your desired discussion should also be included in your meeting confirmation and/ or meeting reconfirmation. Prior to the interview, create a brief agenda and email it to your interviewer. Give one to three talking points at most, but no more than five.

Finally, give the meeting a title. These executives are busy people with packed schedules, so they need a visual confirmation of what the meeting is about right in their calendar. Possible examples are "Accessing and penetrating the South-Korean market," "Expansion in Asia," or "Turnaround of ABC Business."

Now, you are all set. Both parties are aligned about the meeting topics. And your counterpart knows who he or she will be talking to.

MEETING FOLLOW-UP

Your job is not done once the meeting is over. To fully command the interview, you must correctly follow up afterwards to move forward in the hiring process.

Correct follow up means that you thank all the parties you spoke with, repeat the main meeting outcomes, and, most importantly, ask for next steps in the process or reconfirm what has been agreed upon as the next steps. Essentially, who does what by when should be addressed in your follow up message.

> **Drive the process, don't lean back.**

A follow-up is crucial to confirm, present your case to the next decisionmaker, or start a procedure that will lead to your hiring.

You probably realize that this is remarkably similar to the effective communication of any premium brand salesperson. There is nothing new here. Executives who do job search for the first time, are out of the market for several years, or are only accustomed to the Open Job Market recruitment scenario need to adapt swiftly to a more proactive role for success in the Hidden Job Market video interview process. And you can do this by actively motivating others to take the necessary action and creating a win-win situation for everyone.

4. STORYTELLING VIA VIDEO

You've hooked the interviewer and laid the groundwork with an introduction that establishes your control and has focused attention on you. Now, it is time to actually tell your story. Developing your story's content in an optimal way is essential to a successful pitch because it provides the evidence that will convince your interviewer to act in response to the final step—the Call to Action.

> *"Those who tell stories rule society."* —Plato

As you will see below, many storytelling formats follow a similar pattern; the goal is not to find the "perfect" storytelling format but to find the one that best works for you. An ideal storytelling format gives structure to your stories and gets the point across quickly and clearly without wasting your (or the interviewer's) precious time.

MEAT ON THE BONE

Meat on the Bone, another element of the Morita Method, is about supplying proof (the "meat") by giving examples, providing numbers, or listing your accomplishments after you have hooked the audience and introduced yourself with your value claim. Meat on the Bone as a concept is centered on layering evidence upon the value framework established by your introduction. It is used to quickly express the necessary evidence to back up your overall value claim and to get to the heart of your qualifications without an exhaustive run through your entire resume.

Without Meat on the Bone, the interviewer will get back to you with unexpected and potentially unpleasant questions in order to verify your claims, wasting precious time during your pitch.

Meat on the Bone can guide your strategy for fleshing out your interview pitch. The goal should be to stick to the absolute minimum necessary to convey confidence in your idea and provide evidence that your approach will work.

You should keep the concept of Meat on the Bone in mind as we explore the two storytelling formats I suggest for developing your content successfully.

USING A STORYTELLING FORMAT

You may or may not be a natural storyteller; even if you are, the stories you excel at telling may not have the same form and function as the stories you need to tell successfully during a pitch. What you do have, however, is a story to tell. And what you need is an appropriate storytelling format that allows this story to do its job: support your pitch with incontrovertible evidence.

THE STAR FORMAT

STAR stands for Situation, Task, Action, Result, and the STAR format is commonly taught to MBA students as a means to respond to behavioural interview questions. You probably know the kind well: "What was your biggest failure on the job?"; "Describe a time when you utilized your knowledge/experience to solve a problem."; and so on.

The STAR format was designed with these questions in mind. In telling a story using this format, you spend a short amount of time describing the Situation you were faced with (to clarify its fit to the interviewer's question), then you identify the specific Task you were given. These two expository elements should usually take little more than a quarter of the total time spent on the story, while the majority of your time is then spent on the Action section, describing what you did, your thought process or rationale for those actions, and finally a short note on the Result.

THE CAR FORMAT

The second storytelling format has many similarities with the first. CAR stands for Challenge, Action, and Result, and this format condenses Situation and Task into one overall phase, which sets the scene for your description of the actions you took to address a particular challenge.

Similar to the STAR format, the CAR format was designed as a framework for answering behavioural interview questions quickly and successfully. It provides you with a way to quickly get to the heart of the matter and not spend an unnecessary amount of time on exposition or on the downstream effects of your actions.

By using one of these storytelling methods, you can supply proof of your value without wasting time or losing your interviewer's interest. Remember, your answers should be no more than two minutes if possible. Short, direct responses will help to ensure your interviewer isn't becoming victim to the power of distraction and missing key points about your Unique Value Proposition.

5. VIDEO PRESENTATION SKILLS

Owning the room can seem difficult to do, especially in our new age of virtual interviewing. However, there are some tips you can use to help keep attention on you and focus on the aspects of your pitch that you seek to highlight.

Being in a video interview is a bit like auditioning for a role. More than being about getting the role, auditioning is about turning the casting director into your biggest fan. After the audition, you have little to no control over what happens, so you must strive to leave a good impression in the time you have.

Just like a professional actor, make yourself the person that people will want to work with by not only getting familiar with the lines but also by tailoring your presentation and positioning for the camera. In other words, the technical aspects of succeeding in a video interview are just as important as the content of your pitch.

SETTING THE STAGE

It is imperative that you make the best first impression you can, even in a video interview. Much like you would never dream of attending an in-person interview in your pajamas and slippers, you must take care that the first impression you project to the interviewer on camera is one of professionalism and competence.

Thus, ensure that your Twitter, Zoom, Teams, or other screen name and photo/avatar are professional and appropriate, as these will be the very first things about you that the interviewer will see. You should also take care to keep your background neutral and professional; don't be afraid to make use of artificial backgrounds in order to ensure consistency without requiring an entire redecorating session in your interviewing space.

Aside from aesthetic considerations, you should take care to check your technology in advance, as well; poor audio and video quality and faulty connections can spell doom for your pitch. If the interviewer can't hear or see you properly, they can't be impressed by what you have to say and are likely to be distracted and irritated instead of thinking about your great ideas for the organization.

We'll talk more on the technical aspects in a later chapter.

BODY LANGUAGE IS STILL CRITICAL, ESPECIALLY ONLINE

By now, most of us have had many online meetings. Haven't you noticed when one of your colleagues was toying with an item at their desk, clearly reading emails, or otherwise disengaged with the conversation? Don't make the mistake of thinking that your interviewer cannot see exactly what you are doing or how you are presenting yourself.

Make use of positive body language by smiling, maintaining eye contact, using hand gestures as appropriate to emphasize your points, and nodding along and otherwise communicating that you are following the conversation.

Remember that video interviews are 90% preparation and just 10% presentation. It's almost never a good idea to simply go off the cuff and engage in a conversation. Instead, memorize your script, study your role, and passionately rehearse your delivery—that way, you'll be closer to being the person who gets the part!

We will revisit the topics of storytelling and video presentation in the following chapters, paying particular attention to the role that passion and authenticity plays in your video interview success.

VIDEO INTERVIEW SUCCESS

CHAPTER 3:
PILLAR 1: TECHNICAL CHOICES

"To be prepared is half the victory."
—Miguel de Cervantes

V ideo interview success requires mastery of the three pillars of video interviewing which are:

> 3 Pillars of Video Interview Success:
> **Pillar 1: Your Technical Choices**
> **Pillar 2: Your Hollywood Setting**
> **Pillar 3: Your Interview Performance**

This book, however, is about success in the Hidden Job Market. Let me emphasize that navigating the Hidden Job Market job interview and, within that, the world of video interviewing is a self-discovery process, which means it is highly personal.

You could say it is both an art and a science. This journey is about finding your own way. Develop your own approach and style for video interviews in the Hidden Job Market to achieve the best interview performance. Ultimately, your interview success is the goal here, not perfecting a certain method for video job interviews.

On this journey, let me guide you along the Hidden Job Market path of success. Let me guide you from blending in the particular factors producing success, but also failure for hidden opportunities. The aim of this book is to be your guide for Hidden Job Market scenarios. I would be surprised if you would not become a much better performer for open jobs along the way. This also means that when talking about the 3 Pillars of video interviewing, I will blend in my Hidden Job Market perspective.

PILLAR 1: TECHNICAL CHOICES
TECHNICAL PREPARATION FOR A VIDEO INTERVIEW

You know how you express great awe after watching a movie with perfect graphics, video, and sound quality? It is obvious that a lot of work went into the production process and the choice of technology to enable optimal movie quality. The director and cinematographer didn't just arrive on set and begin shooting. It doesn't work that way.

Instead, the cinematographer needs to put every aspect of the movie production in order, so as to have a production that reflects the intention of the director. After having full grasp of the project, the cinematographer then swings into action to prepare a gear list for the production.

From the set selection to the choice of lighting, the use of teleprompters and cameras—cinematographers make sure they have all the necessary equipment before filming starts. Not only that, they also do a few test shots. For instance, they want to know if the video angles are appropriate and if the sound comes out loud and clear. Cinematographers know that audiences often demand movies with novel special effects which come from leveraging technology and particular software.

The same is true for video interviews.

Therefore, I have taken a deeper look at the role of software in enabling you to deliver a winning video interview performance. Just like cinematographers, as a job-seeking executive, you also need to make sure you prepare and test your equipment before you participate in an interview. Otherwise, you may find yourself in a messy situation.

Just because you don't have to leave your home doesn't mean you shouldn't prepare. In fact, your next job might depend on how well you are able to put your right foot and best face forward to impress the interviewers on the other side of the video call. Here are a range of technical tips to help you become masterful at digital interviewing.

#1: WHEN TOO MUCH TECHNOLOGY CREATES A PROBLEM

Beware of using technology to create a trap of your own making. Interactive smart devices may disturb you or even interfere with your interview. Let me give you an example.

An American executive interviewed an Italian executive. At the beginning of the interview, they started to talk about towns famous for their beaches. The Italian mentioned Rimini. All of a sudden, they heard somebody say: "I will call Dr. Rimini." The Italian executive was so surprised to hear the voice of Siri and said: "Don't call Dr. Rimini." Siri replied: "Understood, I won't."

Such a case was relatively harmless. But how would you feel if you were in an interview and the interviewer said, "Shall I send you a message now?" and Siri responds with "Do you want a massage?" That would be embarrassing! Such embarrassments can easily cost you the interview.

Siri is Apple's digital assistant, and Alexa is the one of Amazon. Google Assistant is a virtual assistant software application developed by Google that is primarily available on mobile and home automation devices. Based on artificial intelligence, Google Assistant can engage in two-way conversations.

Toys for children also tend to be interactive these days. Don't leave anything to chance. Make sure that voice recognition and interpretation systems in your room or the smart devices carrying them are switched off.

> **Switch your mobile phone off before the video interview to avoid any disturbing interference.**

Let me repeat my message here since old habits are difficult to change and require repetition: Don't leave anything to chance.

You often see movies with people in front of the computer, and then suddenly, the phone rings. Be it a call from a doctor confirming your COVID-19 test appointment or your social media app sending you a push notification, you cannot afford such disruptions to leak through to your Hollywood-grade movie shooting of a video interview.

While you are preparing for a fight with a dragon, a small mosquito may kill you or cause serious harm. In other words, the real risk may come from things or habits you are not thinking about. Now you know how to eliminate that risk in terms of your video interview.

#2 TESTING

A golden rule of success for any part of your video interview is to test the technology before going live.

As you probably know, a video interview normally takes place via a videoconferencing app or platform. Therefore, you must download the app, test it to be sure it is compatible with your device, and familiarize yourself with the technology before the scheduled interview. You should do a test run as far as the system will let you do a test run.

If a test is not fully possible, then you can also watch a YouTube video about how to boot and use the application. It's important to familiarize yourself with the software as much as you can because don't want to get in the middle of the interview and start looking for a feature you should have discovered in advance (i.e., screen sharing, turning your camera on, etc.).

In addition to testing the application or software you will be using, it is also essential to test the link you created or were provided for the meeting. Never assume that meeting links you receive or create will work. Only after clicking on them will you know for sure.

Some applications might only allow you to test the link up to a certain point, depending on how far out you are from the scheduled meeting. For example, with Google Hangouts or Microsoft Teams, you will only be able to reach the stage where the software tells you to wait until the interviewer lets you in. If you come that far, then you can rest assured that the link is working and active.

By taking the time to do this, you have reduced the chance of a link-not-working-surprise failure. And that's required for each video interview.

Testing is the most neglected element among all interviewees, and more often than not, it is the leading factor for poor video interview performance.

> **Lack of testing is the biggest source of underperformance in video interviews.**

Remember what I previously said: Good is no longer good enough. If you do not test, how do you expect to improve at video interviewing?

One possible reason is that people, in private and possibly in business, are troubleshooting only when things seriously escalate. Why bother troubleshooting if nothing is wrong? Most people are used to solving issues when they arise and thus have developed a certain end-of-pipe firefighting attitude.

The same attitude is adopted for videoconference technology. People assume that these applications work. They have blind trust in technology "running the show" and regard it as a given. This is completely wrong. Check it out first, then rely on it.

As long as you do not take anything for granted or rely on something with blind trust, then you are in a much less vulnerable position. Adopt the mindset that you are lucky if the technology works as promised, but you will also test everything in advance to reduce the likelihood of bad luck.

> **People regard most video meeting software solutions as a given that "simply work." That is very risky—shit happens!**

You run the show. Software is a vital tool that is part of your show, but it needs prior verification.

POTENTIAL PROBLEMS: SOFTWARE UPGRADES, AUTO-UPDATES, AND APPLICATION CRASHES—OH MY!

There are tons of things that can unexpectedly go wrong with your technology before or during a video interview.

For example, your Zoom software may be installed and usually working fine, but, very annoyingly, just one minute before the interview starts, when you click on the job interview video link in hopes of the video interface popping up, you get a notification that your software requires upgrading. And it says it will take about three to five minutes.

You become nervous knowing you will be at least a few minutes late instead of early like you had planned. A simple software test run would have avoided this software upgrade hitting you in the worst moment and causing a serious interview delay.

In the same vein, how do you deal with auto-updates of your machine? I don't know about your computer, but my computer has a bad habit of just doing what it wants when it wants, and usually when I do not want it to. Generally speaking, it's probably safer to make sure that Windows, Apple, or whatever software you use has finished all its latest updates well before an interview.

Another catastrophe comes to mind: Zoom may quit unexpectedly. This could happen while you are booting or later. If it happens when you boot, then your face might turn red and you might say, "How annoying," or "What the hell is going on now?" You may be at a loss for what to do.

Zoom quit unexpectedly

Generate a crash report to help Zoom resolve this problem.

Description

> Briefly describe what happened
>
>
>
>
>
>   400

By clicking "Send to Zoom", you authorize Zoom to access data in this crash report, subject to our Privacy Policy.

☐ Do not ask me again   Don't Send   **Send to Zoom**

Writing a crash report? Certainly not because you are already running late for your interview. The best option is to simply try again. At best, you reboot your computer, close tabs and other applications, try again, and it works, making you five minutes late. At worst, you do the same steps, and it still doesn't work, causing you to ask the interviewer to reschedule.

So, why does this happen, and how can we prevent it?

It could be an issue with Zoom itself, but more likely than not, it is a result of running too many applications on your computer simultaneously. Don't wait for your computer to give out before you close out of applications you aren't actively using. Remember, your computer can only do so much at once, and you want it to focus on what is most important—and in this moment, it is your video interview.

I'd like to now share with you a personal experience I had with Zoom.

For context, Zoom allows users to join without the need to download and install their software. I must admit I used that option too many times with my laptop at home.

One time, while I was on a business trip in Asia, I tried to join a Zoom session in the middle of the night, and it did NOT work. Apparently, the browser on my smart phone was not compatible with this capability. I was unable to join and missed a very important meeting.

It helps to illustrate that we cannot count on such technology to "just work," especially when we change a few things. Sometimes it works as expected, but often, it does not.

We should always remind ourselves, that technology performs well most of the time.

Most problems are not a technology problem but a user problem.

The user does not know how to properly make use of technology.

POTENTIAL SOLUTION: TRIAL RUN WITH A COLLEAGUE, FRIEND, OR FAMILY MEMBER

If you are not used to having a video chat, then you might find a video interview to be slightly awkward at first. Almost everyone on their first attempt has an inclination to look away from the camera, maintain bad posture, fiddle with their hands, or make gestures that appear faintly or are not visible.

What you see in a movie is usually the result of intensive rehearsals. This is a process during which a director prepares their actors for filming. No matter how 'professional' such an actor is, they have to understand their role and how to portray it in front of a camera before the actual production. They also do multiple takes before they successfully capture "the one."

Ideally, you would have considered yourself ready to get on the virtual interview stage, considering your level of preparation and familiarization with face-to-face interviews. However, video interviews are a whole different beast; therefore, I recommend you take some time to practice.

The day before the interview or on the same day several hours before, you should do a trial run so you can see how you look on screen, check your sound, see what your internet speed is, determine how to visibly make your gestures, discover possible technical glitches you might face, and figure out how to quickly fix any issues that may arise, among other things.

And a great way to do this and make it feel more "real" is to do this trial run with someone you know on the other line, whether it's a family member, friend, or colleague. They can give you real feedback about how you look and sound.

> **Do not change anything in your video call set up after the trial.**

The trial should be similar to a final rehearsal of an orchestra before a performance starts. Upon completion of the trial, you should freeze your set up. Minor changes can mess up everything. Therefore, don't change anything. Keep it with the assurance that everything works.

#3 THE VIDEO INTERVIEW CONFIRMATION

In the Hidden Job Market, the job-seeking executive is responsible for orchestrating a successful meeting. That means you need to think of everything to make the video meeting smooth, comfortable, and successful.

And confirming the date and time you agreed on is an important task.

Don't assume that everyone is organized and on top of their schedules. Do your due diligence and send out calendar invitations to hold time for your video meeting. Using scheduling software to send calendar invitations and confirm attendance will help minimize the risk of scheduling errors or conflicts.

> **Sending calendar invitations of the proposed interview helps to reduce scheduling errors.**

In your calendar invitation, include all information the interviewer will need to access the video meeting—namely, the link! Also include your telephone number to revert to in case unforeseen technical issues arise with video.

You are dealing with very busy people. Some of them delegate their schedules to secretaries or virtual assistants which is all the more reason to be on alert when it comes to meeting confirmations. Ascertain that they can easily access your video link.

Sending an email with the link or access details is one way to do this, but there is still the risk of them not being able to find this particular email when they need it, especially if it is hidden in a long email thread.

Let me ask you this: How many times were you unable to find a video meeting link or the necessary access details? Your counterpart will run into similar problems unless you send calendar invitations.

YOU must assure that the interviewer has easy access to your video call link.

MEETING CONFIRMATION VIA SCHEDULING SOFTWARE

Calendar invitations have become industry standards for executives all over the world, so don't forget to send one to your interviewer once the meeting time is set, regardless of the interview medium. He or she can easily respond to the invitation, signaling to you that they either "accept" the invite and are planning to attend or "decline" the invite for one reason or another.

However, when sending a calendar invitation, do not use the word "interview" during the early stages of prospecting a hidden job opportunity, as is presented in the example below.

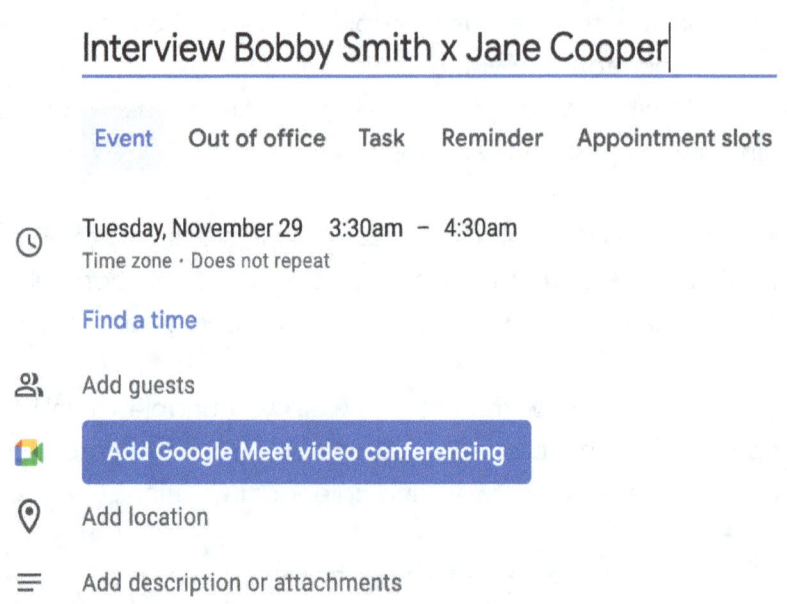

Remember at this stage, you want a business discussion centering around needs analysis and proposing yourself as a best-fit solution to address the company's growth challenges. By suggesting an interview, you are only setting yourself up to be rejected if there are no open positions available.

Instead of using the word "interview" in your meeting invitation, choose a catchy phrase or topic that hits the root canal pains your counterpart is experiencing. For example, a global chief revenue officer based in Switzerland may face stagnant or declining market shares or not have access at all in key export markets such as China, Japan, or South-Korea. Hence, you can title the meeting something like "Access Korean/Japanese Markets" or "Expanding in Korean/Japanese Markets," and the calendar invitation will be accepted with great interest.

Alternatively, if you are already mid-way in the process of engaging decisionmakers at your target company, then there is another way. You can call the appointment "Catch-up," "Follow-up," or simply "Call [Your Name] X [Their Name] on [Software]." In the example below, I've done something similar using a Google Calendar invite, but you can do the same thing on whatever scheduling software you're comfortable with.

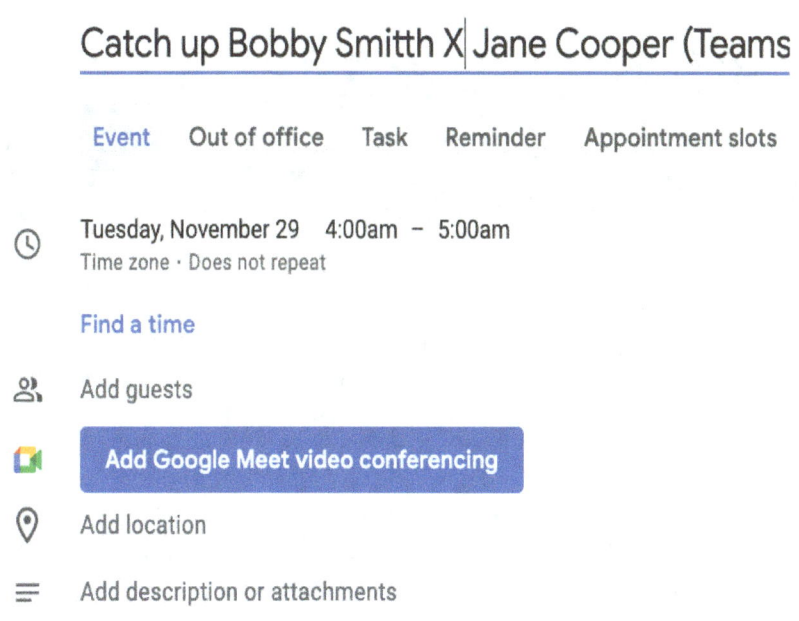

Catch up Bobby Smitth X Jane Cooper (Teams

Event   Out of office   Task   Reminder   Appointment slots

🕐 Tuesday, November 29   4:00am – 5:00am
    Time zone · Does not repeat

    Find a time

👥 Add guests

📹 **Add Google Meet video conferencing**

📍 Add location

☰ Add description or attachments

The point is this: choose other inconspicuous words that do not reveal to your counterpart that you are on an outright job hunt. The most important thing in the Hidden Job Market is to be inconspicuous.

And you must remain inconspicuous until you have identified a potential opportunity inside the company. Then, choose the right timing to call the conversation an "interview" to signal to certain people that you are in this meeting to discuss an executive opportunity inside their company.

OTHER WAYS TO CONFIRM

While calendar invitations and meeting confirmations are pretty standard across the board, you can also confirm with the interviewer via call, text, or social media if the meeting is more informal and depending on how you've been communicating with them up until this point.

In fact, my favorite way is to confirm meetings via telephone.

> **Like no other means, the telephone gives you immediate and full control over the process of scheduling your appointment.**

This gives you maximum control that your counterpart is really available, or if other commitments have popped up, you can quickly adjust the appointment in real time. Why do you think executive search agents around the world often use the telephone? Control.

This approach is also very personal and adds a "high-end" touch to your interactions which makes the counterpart feel valued and appreciated. This is not to be underestimated.

In some cases, however, confirming by telephone is not possible or not desirable, especially when the interviewer is attending major events or on an intensive flight schedule. In that case, let the scheduling software do the job for you automatically. And even if you plan to confirm the meeting via another method, you should still send out a calendar invitation regardless to reduce the chance of the interviewer being double-booked.

#4 CHOOSING THE BEST HARDWARE

Before joining a video interview, you must be sure that you choose the most suitable—and comfortable—device with the right and most reliable technology. This could be anything from a computer to a tablet to a smartphone.

For most interviews, a computer will be best. I advise you to use a desktop computer, ideally with a strong and stable LAN-cable connection or a strong Wi-Fi connection. The reason I prefer a desktop version over a mobile device is two-fold. On the one hand, the mobile device screen is small, and you might miss subtle nuances on the face of the interviewer, which could have come to the fore with a broader screen. On the other hand, I see too many things go wrong with mobile hardware such as moving, shaking, falling down, battery running low, etc.

In most cases, your desktop computer is the cornerstone of your video interview set up. By virtue of being tied to a specific location, you improve all aspects of your desktop technology choices. Ultimately, it offers the technically illiterate person more success in a Hollywood-grade video shooting set up and, therefore, the highest chances of delivering an impeccable video interview performance.

However, make sure your computer is relatively modern and updated. Old computer hardware may be too weak to handle the latest video conferencing systems. This could cause a variety of problems such as poor image quality, poor sound quality, short battery life, overheating, etc.

Check: Does your computer take more than a minute to restart?

It's of course unacceptable that any executive has a computer that takes more than a minute to restart. It should be fixed immediately as a first step in technical preparation.

In your own interest, though, check before the interview that not only the hardware but also the software for your video interview works without a problem given the hardware specification of your machine.

Addressing this problem in detail goes beyond the scope of this book; therefore, I will only provide some general advice. You can check this yourself if you are computer savvy. Otherwise, you should ask IT or computer experts to assess your hardware/software choices and point out any potential issues.

MOBILE DEVICES

I don't recommend using a mobile device for a video interview, but sometimes, it is inevitable. In that case you need to take the following precautions:

- Position the camera of your mobile device at or slightly above the eyebrows to avoid looking down at the screen.
- Mount the mobile device with another device so that it does not shake, move, or fall off.
- Ensure the device is charged prior to the interview. You should also avoid running low on battery by planning to have it plugged in throughout the session.
- Shut down any programs that might interrupt the process before the interview starts.
- Make sure your Wi-Fi reception is strong enough at your chosen location.
- Check that your sound and background are fine.
- Download any plugins that may help in seeing you through a hitch-free video interview process. Plugins are internet browser extensions that help to improve the functionality of an application.
- Turn on "Do not disturb" or a similar notification silencer application if it is available on your device.

Note that incoming phone calls or incoming messages may interfere with your interview, putting your entire job interview at risk. More often than not, this is completely outside of your control. Choose a computer, laptop, or tablet to be on the safer side.

> **Incoming phone calls or messages are putting your video interview at risk.**

Even if you have to use your mobile device, avoid in-car interviews at all costs. They put your video experience at even more risk. Think of how little you can control from things like sunlight and sound to internet speed and having an "on the road" image. You simply cannot control the environment surrounding your car.

#5 VIDEO SOFTWARE

What video meeting solutions are out there?

The answer is mind-boggling—too many! For the purpose of this book, I will not review any solutions for the same reasons I do not cover other IT issues. A general discussion will suffice.

I find the number of video meeting solutions currently available to be overwhelming. Zoom, for example, lists 46 competing applications on their site.

It is good for you to know the main ones which are Zoom, Microsoft Teams, Google Meet, Facetime, and Cisco WebEx. Skype used to be one of the pioneers and has high name recognition, but it has fallen behind competition in recent years. LinkedIn Video Calling is another option, but it is not a standalone software as it is integrated into the LinkedIn communication system and therefore often overseen.

In an article published by Capermint, I quickly discovered that there are much more video calling and chatting apps out there than I know. The incomplete list captures 26 of them.

Google Meet	Facetime
Facebook Messenger	Skype
Zoom Meetings	Microsoft Teams
Discord	Google Meet
WhatsApp	Cisco Webex
Whereby	Google Hangout
Instagram	Snapchat
Telegram	Signal Private Messenger
IMO	Jio Chat
WeChat	LINE Messenger
Viber Messenger	ICQ New
Houseparty	Squad Video Chat
JusTalk	ooVoo

Source: https://www.capermint.com/blog/top-26-free-video-chat-apps/

CHOOSE YOUR VIDEO CALLING SOFTWARE WISELY!

"Video calling is an amazing way to connect with everyone and have a face-to-face interaction," writes the Capermint team in their review of video calling software. I would add the following phrase: if you make it so.

> Video calling is an amazing way to connect with everyone and have a face-to-face interaction, **if you make it so.**

I emphasize that an amazing video call experience does not happen automatically. You need to make it happen. The software is the tool, but you are the enabler. You need to be familiar with the use of video calling software so that you can effortlessly deliver an impeccable interview experience.

And selecting the right video calling software is a step that most job-seekers neglect.

Other books claim the only thing you need to be able to do is open the video interview call link sent by the hiring company, but that is the Open Job Market scenario where the interviewer is expected to set up the interview.

In the Hidden Job Market, though, you must often propose video calls, set them up as smoothly as possible, and manage the whole experience flawlessly. And you can't rely on excuses, such as, "Oh, I didn't know that," or "This is new to me. Let me check this out later." You do not get a second chance to create a winning first impression.

> **Determine one to two video calling softwares which are best for you and keep optimizing them for your purpose.**

Video conferencing solutions are quickly evolving and will keep you busy with new features and system upgrades. Whether you want it or not, the software will change, and you need to be on top of it.

Decide first on which software solution creates the best interview experience for the interviewer with impeccable quality. Some softwares have free versus premium paid-for options, so you'll need to determine if you have a budget and what that budget is. Ask around, consider the advice of video interviewing experts or video shooting professionals, and read online video calling software reviews. Ultimately, select your top two video applications. You need to be able to offer more than one application in case your counterpart is not able to use your favorite choice.

There are two more aspects you might not consider. If you frequently travel, check whether your video solution works in those regions or countries you are travelling to or if there are ways to make them work despite technical restrictions. For the international travelling executive, note that in China and the United Arab Emirates, many video software apps are blocked and hence do not work. In China, the Chinese app WeChat is a reliable option.

In the United Arab Emirates, you need a VPN. VPN stands for Virtual Private Network. As long as you get yourself access to a VPN you can use most apps, but testing prior to use is essential.

Secondly, check whether you understand the privacy policy that comes along with the software provided. In 2023, Zoom for example released its new privacy policy. Zoom built into its privacy policy your consent that they can record any of your Zoom meetings and use those recordings for product development or business creation of any kind. Given the confidential nature of your interview communication, you need to be cautious. Zoom also feeds any contact information of yours into their database if you give them your consent. That means if you do not withdraw your consent, your contact information will be sold under the Zoom database service brand. Be cautious. Do not blindly trust technology providers.

After investigating, analyzing, and assessing the different options available to you, make a choice and customize your top two software solutions to your preferences.

> **Customization is key because you want to look not just good, but great.**

Optimizing the interview experience by customizing preferences inside the video conferencing software is something I do all the time. The use of artificial background is an important choice. Make sure your software offers this feature if an artificial background is your preferred way to go.

The good thing about Hidden Job Market interviews is that often you are the one who is taking the initiative to propose interviews, and, therefore, the choice of software is yours, whereas in Open Job Market interviews, the interviewer often dictates the setting. Use this control to your advantage to create the best possible interview set up and delivery.

#6: KEEP IT PROFESSIONAL, EVEN WITH THE LITTLE DETAILS!

Unfortunately, the first impression a video interviewer has of you in the video interview space is not your face or real body image; rather, it is your username, your profile picture, and your background (real or virtual).

These may seem like minor details, but they are actually a pretty big deal and shouldn't be taken lightly.

YOUR ACCOUNT AND USERNAME

First and foremost, do not use someone else's account—even if it's your wife's or your child's. You want to have your own account, so it isn't confusing for the interviewer at any point in the process.

If the software you use requires a username, make sure it is simple and professional, even if you don't think anyone will ever see it. It's better to be safe than sorry.

Next, take a look at your screen name, which most video conferencing softwares allow you to change and customize even beyond the username. Anything besides your first and last names—including numbers, usernames, and nick names—is confusing to the interviewer and will cause a small ditch in his or her excitement levels. It's not professional nor is it a good first impression.

Keep it simple and professional and change your screen name to display as "First and Last Name" only.

YOUR PROFILE PHOTO

Create a winning first impression of your video interview with an impressive professional photo or avatar inside the video conferencing system or video app. This works great as a precursor to the real version of yourself appearing when you are fully live.

> **Your photo or avatar today is like your job interview outfit 30 years ago.**

In the same way that people are making a poor impression on LinkedIn with a casual LinkedIn photo or no photo at all, a casual or nonexistent video conferencing photo or avatar is a disappointment for the interviewer.

Teddy Burris, a LinkedIn strategist, said, "Many recruiters have said to me, 'Not having a LinkedIn Profile photo indicates you are not approachable'."

Now, I cannot claim you are not approachable because of not having a photo, but I can assure you that you create an emotional disconnect with your counterpart.

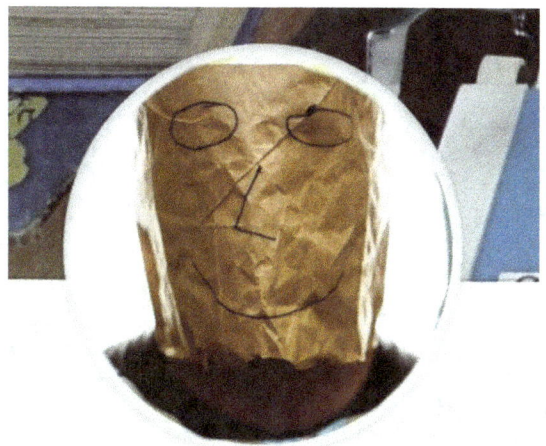

Courtesy: Teddy Burris, Printed with permission.

When choosing a photo, make sure it is a professional headshot and not a casual or satiric one used in social media like Facebook/Meta or WhatsApp where you connect with friends.

Also, do not use your company logo. You are not promoting your company's brand; you are promoting yourself.

And finally, this should go without saying, but don't use technical gadget images like the example below which looks like a web camera.

One of my clients, who was a candidate for a CEO position, used this image and had a terrible experience with it. The first minute after logging in, the interviewers heard his voice asking: "Can you see me?" His video camera wasn't working for some reason, so the interviewers only saw this web camera image. You can imagine that the interviewers got a bad first impression and had cold feet because of this technical glitch but even more so because of the immature photo they saw in the executive's place. Don't let that be you.

YOUR BACKGROUND

For reasons of authenticity, a real background is always preferable to a virtual background. If you are travelling or if your real background is not appropriate to show and you don't have time to make changes, then opt for a digital solution.

Popular video conferencing apps including Zoom offer virtual backgrounds in the app. You can also download virtual backgrounds online and import them into the video conferencing application. You can choose from a wide range of backgrounds. See below for some effective virtual background examples.

Virtual backgrounds are a good way to project professionalism even if you are in an unprofessional setting. Nobody will know what is behind or surrounding you in reality. It's also an easy way to go, especially if you don't want to go through the long process of making extensive changes to your home. My candidate still has the Simpson cartoon on his wall and can enjoy video calls with his virtual setting.

Here is one important rule for selecting the right backgrounds: The background must first and foremost appeal to the interviewer. You are second.

> **The perceived value of the background is in the eye of the interviewer.**

Don't select and upload images from WhatsApp, Instagram, or Facebook/Meta because you find them "cool." This is the wrong approach. "What's in it for them?" should be your first question. "What's in for me?" should be your second question. A good choice is satisfying the requirements of both worlds.

Consider virtual backgrounds that resonate with the target company or interviewer. If you check that box, then you should make sure the background reflects your personal preferences as well.

The variety of images you can choose from is unlimited, but I want you to select one, maximum two images, and focus. You need to focus on and optimize one background. This in itself is an improvement project.

Focus on one virtual background, not several, and then make it look great for your particular video interview case.

Notice how people react to your chosen setting. Let their reaction guide you for further possible improvements of making the image smaller, bigger, darker, brighter, or other technical enhancements.

The Morita Method Executive must be mobile at any moment, whether you like it or not. You may not be an internationally travelling executive, but you still need a portable system. I can't even count how many times I've experienced internet interruptions and needed to move elsewhere at short notice. Think of making your entire video interview system portable or you create a problem of your own making. In this world of disruption, being ready for your video interview wherever, whenever is a big plus.

#7: VIDEO QUALITY

While video quality in a video interview setting is mostly out of the user's control, there are a few ways you can improve it and make it more effective for your purposes.

LIGHTING

Lighting used in movie production helps to create a visual mood as well as communicate a sense of meaning to the audience. Depending on how it is set, it can make or break a scene. The same thing applies to video interviews. The lighting system you use determines in part how the interviewers will perceive you.

Of course, you want to use good lighting so the interviewer can see you clearly. In this case, light from natural sources is preferable. However, be sure that the sun doesn't shine in the direction of your eyes so it doesn't make you squint. In the absence of a natural light source, you may consider an artificial lighting system such as fluorescent or ring lights. If you'll be making use of lamps, test out different setups to make sure they shine evenly across your face.

CONSIDER AN EXTERNAL CAMERA
Your video camera and the quality of image resolution determines whether the images seen by the interviewer are impeccable, average, or unclear. We can all agree here: There is no faster way to ruin your interview than a blurred image or low image resolution.

For this reason, you should have a reliable camera to capture high quality footage.

Computer-integrated cameras are getting better and better. External webcams however still deliver much better image resolution and are an excellent option for most executives.

Usually, during peak Internet traffic hours, your image quality deteriorates, if not freezes. The same might happen during bad weather conditions such as heavy rain or snowfalls. In this case, a strong, reliable internet connection will have a positive effect on image quality. To be on the safe side, though, I would schedule your video interview during off-peak

Internet traffic hours and good weather conditions.

POSITION AND ANGLES

The next often-neglected aspect of video quality is the position of the video camera, especially when using an external camera. It should be centred in the middle of the screen and slightly above eye level. Avoid positioning the camera above your head or below your eyes.

In video productions, the head-on frontal view is used to create a scenario that makes a character feel engaged with the subject. Keep an appropriate distance to the camera. Check if your face sits in the middle of the resulting video image, and if not, make slight shifts until it does.

You must verify that your web camera is properly fixed and correctly positioned as part of your pre-interview audit. It is not uncommon for people to touch external webcams or webcam cables and forget to fix and reposition it accurately with the necessary attention. You don't want to be fiddling with this once you are already in the interview.

#8: THE IMPORTANCE OF AUDIO QUALITY

When the interviewer hears your voice for the first time, do you sound great? Or do you suffer from poor audio? If you are watching a movie with low audio quality, then you would be easily distracted by poor sound quality, no matter how brilliant the movie is.

Most people don't even think about how they sound. Why bother? In the digital age with the widespread use of in-ear earbuds and built-in computer microphones, we assume that things are "OK." Things are unfortunately not "OK."

A lot of video conference users generate poor sound quality because they have a poor Wi-Fi connection. Again, your interviewer is disappointed to hear that your voice is choppy or getting cut off. While interviewers don't admit it, nobody enjoys poor audio, and it can severely distract them from you and whatever you are trying to say.

As a way to ensure you have quality sound, use a simple LAN cable to your router, instead of a wireless connection. Then, test your audio settings with someone else before the interview. Also, during the test and interview, be sure to speak clearly, project your voice, and check volume controls throughout.

For the highest quality audio, you may also consider using an external lapel microphone (directly attached to your clothing). Lavalier microphones, also known as lapel mics or clip-on mics, are small, wired microphones widely used in filmmaking and broadcasting. They are ideal for recording dialogue as they are discreet and unobtrusive and can be positioned close to the mouth while remaining out of sight. This may be complemented with wired or wireless earbuds to hear the other person(s).

Some executives asked me what I think about headsets. I think there is no right or wrong answer to this question, but I dare to say that the overwhelming majority of high profile business leaders in the world, especially when they go live in front of audiences, tend to hide microphones as much as possible. I have never seen any publicly listed company CEO with a headset.

Some people argue that a headset may look as if you are playing video games in your basement as opposed to being a Global Fortune 500 Executive. I do not share this opinion. And I believe that it is totally acceptable to wear headsets to enjoy superior sound and shut out the influence of outer noise. Not everyone will notice or be distracted by your headset, but everyone will notice and be distracted by your poor quality audio.

#9: YOUR INTERNET SPEED MATTERS

Video conferencing tools have internet requirements for sending and receiving high-definition video to ensure a seamless call experience. A poor connection will be disastrous to your cause, especially if you're the only one facing such technical issues. You don't want to be cut out half-way through. It is therefore recommended that you go with the 2.4 GHz signal standard.

If you aren't sure what your Wi-Fi speed is, check online for free Wi-Fi speed testing websites. These will check your speed for you, so you can decide if you need to call your provider and upgrade to a better speed.

If your Wi-Fi signals aren't strong, consider joining the interview from a place where you can get a stronger signal. As a measure to improve speeds, consider turning off other devices in your house which are connected to the same network. Also, close all apps running in the background. This could be anything from file-sharing programs to any other apps that seem to be using a part of your bandwidth.

TIME LAGS MIGHT BE INEVITABLE

The reality is that, despite your preparation, you may still face some glitches. Your computer could freeze. Your microphone or camera might be defective. Above all, you may face a delay, hearing what the interviewer has said a few moments later.

In this case, try to avoid speaking over your interviewer. You should learn to practice patience as the delay might be a result of an internet glitch or device freeze. In other words, when you feel the person on the other side of the camera has finished speaking, take a beat before you respond. You don't want to cut your interviewers off and be rude even if you weren't intentional about it.

#10: OTHER WAYS TO PREPARE

There are a few final technical tips I'd like to share with you to help execute a flawless video interview experience.

START EARLY

I shouldn't have to say this, but I do: Why should you be late for a video interview? You don't have to commute or ask for descriptions from passers-by to find the location. Folks, you've simply got no reason to be late. Even professional actors understand the implications of arriving late for movie shoots. One mishap like that and they may suddenly get replaced. They, therefore, try as much as possible to avoid running late to set. When you are running late for the interview, the interviewer is getting cold feet.

> **Trash your telephone call mindset. You tend to underestimate the time to connect with a video call.**

Unlike the telephone which connects the moment you pick up the phone, video conferencing software solutions take time to set up—and you need to factor this time in. For one, you might have to search for the invitation link somewhere in your overflowing email box. Then, you will have to boot the software and input your username and password. All of these things make this process annoying and time-consuming.

Additionally, video communication software tends to consume a lot of internet bandwidth and memory which can cause all sorts of technical issues such as poor sound or video quality, overheating, or even a complete crash. Adding up all these unforeseen things, the average executive with the telephone call mindset only begins the video software initiation process one or two minutes before the interview.

To be on time, be ahead of time!

As the saying goes, to be on time is to be late. So, to be on time, be ahead of time! Finish everything that has to do with preparing for your video interview 15 minutes before the interview starts.

If all goes according to plan, you should be ready in about five minutes. Then, you can take a 10-minute break. If something unexpected happens, then you have time to take corrective action.

Once you're about five minutes out from the interview time, I recommend joining the link, turning your camera on, and waiting patiently for others to join. This will ensure you can greet them when they arrive and start the meeting promptly.

KNOW YOUR LOG IN INFORMATION

We all know how annoying log in issues can be. However, they are completely avoidable. Here are a few ways to reduce log in troubles:

1. Check your log in information before your interview to make sure it's correct
2. Store your credentials in a way that is readily available to you
3. Input the log in information correctly

I know this sounds like common sense, but it's easy when you're in a hurry or anxious about the upcoming interview to skip or mess up some of these simple yet crucial steps.

For example, if you copy the password as presented in the example below, then it will not work. Why? Because you will be copying the extra space at the end. The devil is in the details.

DGKNDODNF8J4·¶

I hate typing passwords like anyone else, but typing passwords by hand or saving them and letting the system automatically insert it will save you time and unnecessary friction.

HAVE A PLAN IN PLACE—SHIT HAPPENS!

I encourage you to embrace the "If I am lucky" mindset because the moment you boot your video application software, many unexpected things may happen. I do not want to go into detail here, but I will mention one incident which happens quite frequently: computers crashing.

As long as you are joining early, you should still have a small time buffer to resolve the issues and be on time. If for any reason you risk a serious delay of more than three minutes, I would take the courtesy of contacting the interviewer. Calling in this situation is better than email. The purpose is to notify him or her that you will be online soon despite some technical issues you are encountering.

So, interrupt your troubleshooting to notify the interviewer. If the problems you are facing are unsurmountable, go as far as proposing to reschedule the interview.

Some people get lost in troubleshooting mode and realize 15 minutes after the planned interview start that they forgot to let the interviewer know what was going on. And this can create a terrible first impression.

The "If I am lucky" mindset is all the more important because some problems are caused—and now comes the surprise—by the interviewer. You would probably never think that the interviewer would be the one messing up the video call, but as you know, shit happens!

NO AUDIO SHEETS

As previously said, the Morita Method Executive must plan ahead and take preparations for what might go wrong on the interviewer's end. "No Audio Sheets" are a great way to plan ahead and help your interviewer troubleshoot issues.

Let us take the case of your interviewer not being able to hear your voice. An awkward sound problem. What would you do in such an emergency situation?

While your first inclination might be to chat them in the video conferencing software, text their cell, or use other chat systems like WhatsApp, this might not be the most effective or efficient way to handle the situation.

My experience has taught me that people using video software are too nervous to even think about using chatting systems. So the use of chat systems is problematic to help you quickly in such an emergency situation.

Instead, I recommend using "No Audio Sheets." Let me explain.

In order to connect with the interviewer if your sound issues prevent you from speaking to him directly, it is ideal that you have prepared written notes in huge not to be overseen capital letters on two or three sheets of white paper. The messages can be as simple as:

- I CANNOT HEAR YOU!
- REBOOT YOUR ZOOM APP
- CALL ME AT 0041 76 538 8989
- CHECK YOUR MICROPHONE SETTINGS
- SEND ME AN MS TEAMS LINK VIA EMAIL

You can write whatever message you need to on a blank sheet of paper when the occasion arises. There are a few examples in the appendix.

If shit happens, and you, the interviewee, have prepared "No Audio Sheets" and save the interviewer from pain, disappointment, embarrassment, and awkwardness, then this will be a major plus for you.

CHAPTER 3 CHEAT SHEET
TECHNICAL CHOICES

This is a list of action items to elevate your technical choices for optimal video interview performance.

DOWNLOAD THE CHEAT SHEET
ON TECHNICAL CHOICES HERE:

www.hiddenexecutivejobs.com/video-interviews

CHAPTER 4:
PILLAR 2: YOUR HOLLYWOOD SETTING

*"Your video setting is similar to the setting of a movie.
Great setting, great movie. Great video interview setting,
great interview impact."*
—Rainer Maria Morita

Hollywood movies have a carefully chosen setting that best fits the movie. Similarly, you need to create or choose a setting that best fits your video interview. Why?

If executives can learn anything from Hollywood, it is the perfection they have developed for modern-day motion pictures and the actors performing in them. Hollywood is synonymous with turning a nobody into a star. Such actors become million dollar brands and buzz agents for their products—the movies. And there is a reason for this. It is the frame that they have spun around their actors—a frame that determines image and reputation.

Hollywood meticulously designs and manages perception. One way is through carefully selecting the setting which I consider the frame of a movie. Great setting, great movie.

Start doing the same for your video interviews—create the frame.

With the internet and new technologies available, never has it been so easy, affordable, and doable for any executive to transform even a dusty old junk room into a million-dollar global player CEO office.

Great video interview setting, great video interview frame, great value perception, great interview impact. Poor setting, poor frame, poor video interview impact.

So, what do I mean by setting?

With setting I refer to anything that your camera captures and shows on the screen to the other side. Executives often focus only on their upper body and neglect what is behind, next to, or above them. Especially when interviewing from home, you should transform your office into an impressive video interview shooting venue. This requires time, energy, and possibly some small investments.

This will definitively require experimenting. And even more importantly, this will require asking others for feedback so you know how they perceive your setting.

Let's talk about some of the best ways to create your perfect video interview "setting."

#1: BE CONSCIOUS OF WHAT IS IN VIEW

Irrespective of where you'll be interviewing, try to make your location communicate professionalism and neutrality as much as possible. Never randomly select your background.

Hollywood movie directors take the upmost scrutiny in selecting their backgrounds, so you should too. Remember that an interview is meant to give the interviewers an opportunity to learn more about you and how you rightly fit into the executive position for which you're interviewing.

The interviewer is there to listen to you, and of course, see you. So, you wouldn't want to give them any chance to get distracted or put off by what you have in your background.

Let me give you some examples. Consider how the interviewer will perceive your suitability for a C-suite position if you have:

- laundry piles in the background
- a messy office desk
- full ashtrays with matches, empty Coca Cola bottles, or several coffee mugs on the table behind you

Remove anything that distracts the interviewer from you, especially very colorful objects in a color neutral environment. Even the chair back is disturbing if it stands out behind your shoulders. Get a chair without a chairback; this is also much healthier for your spine.

As we discussed previously, the power of distraction is one of your biggest challenges in a video interview. When distracted, even briefly, the interviewer may not catch all the details of what you are sharing, causing them to miss valuable insights. And while you can't prevent them from being distracted by everything, you can prevent them from being distracted by your set up with a dedicated interview space free of clutter, distracting décor, and other eye-catching objects.

Even without a dedicated space, you can still set the stage for a distraction-free interview. You don't have to fret over how your home looks. However, convincing your employer that you have great organizational skills starts with the way you present yourself and your environment.

Even in an organized space, take a moment to review what's present in your camera frame.

For example, books can send the wrong message if the book titles create issues with the interview audience such as defamation theories, tantra or sex education, extreme religious topics, war heroes, and so on.

Keep any pets or kids away from the interview room, and inform people at home about the interview so they don't wander or interrupt you with their presence during the process. Even if you tell them, you better put a "DO NOT DISTURB" or "MEETING IN PROGRESS" sign on the door.

CASE: Big Cactus

One executive client of mine has a big, tall cactus in the background. It is clearly visible on the left side of the screen. When I asked my client whether he always had the cactus there, he said, "Yes, certainly, in the end it's my home. So what?" Sure, you can convince yourself it is your home and things like this don't matter.

Then I asked, "What's the general image you associate with a cactus?" He responded, "It hurts."

"Yes, you are right," I said. Then, I shouted, "Yes, it hurts!" He couldn't help but laugh. It was too obvious. He understood his blunder.

The cactus poses a possible risk to get hurt, to experience pain. It is a plant you definitively do not want to touch or connect with. You'd rather avoid or distance yourself from it. In other words, the cactus was sending underlying signals sabotaging his efforts to connect and engage through the digital screen.

My client was planning to have an interview with a CEO at the end of his fifties who was known to be rather conservative. Since the cactus could create negative feelings on the side of the interviewer, I advised him to remove the cactus out of sight.

Take a look at the photo below. How does it feel now? I bet it does not hurt anymore. Can we agree that it is almost neutral?

As a next possible improvement, you can use the neutral space in the background to display an image or logo that fits the interview scenario and company you are interviewing with. I advised my client to put a poster on the wall with an airplane because he was interviewing for an opportunity in the aviation industry.

"But this means faking it. I am not that passionate about airplanes. What happens if he finds out?" he asked.

"He won't. He will not have the time for that in the first interview," I replied.

After re-arranging furniture and wall paintings/posters, it looked very decent and, most importantly, showed airplanes in the background in a subtle way.

It is exaggerated to claim that this small improvement will be recognized by the interviewer as a major factor. But it helps to boost the candidate's image in being perceived as closer or in "the right zone" as a cultural fit for an association related to aviation. This was a highly effective tactic, especially in this case where the candidate's lack of industry experience was a weak point in comparison to other candidates.

It had another positive effect in boosting the candidate's confidence even before the interview began. After the interview, he said, "Went well. I could not do better. Airplanes were a hit (good call)!"

───── CASE: Huge Scary Shark ─────

I will never forget a video interview with a female jobseeker who had a very charming and loving presence (face, smile, voice). Overall, she's what I call a winning presence for a female candidate.

When I asked her about her background, she was surprised because she had not paid attention to it. She had randomly selected a seat in her house. Dominating her background was a very big picture of a huge shark with menacing shark teeth. Like this:

Wow, this scary picture makes you want to escape right away. The main point, though, is that she was not aware of this scary shark as a disturbing element. Without knowing it, she was making a fool out of herself. After I explained to her, we both burst out in laughter and were laughing many minutes because the scene was so ridiculous.

Since what is behind you can be a source of more engagement or disengagement, you should make sure you wear your background. This simply means that you should maintain a professional background.

A good approach to maintaining a background that suggests "professional appropriateness" is to keep it simple—think of interviewing in front of a blank or neutral wall.

Alternatively, you can create a background that tells more about who you are and what you do, as long as it is in relation to the position you're interviewing for.

Finally, if you feel your living situation may get in the way of your level of confidence during the interview process, then you may consider the use of a virtual background that at least suggests you're in a home office.

CASE: Global Marketing Director Video Interview

In the final round for a global marketing director position, a client of mine had a video interview with two interviewers. The overall impression of the interviewee was good. He was able to answer all questions and was well qualified. Everything went smoothly.

However, the interviewers rejected him. As negative feedback, he received the following comment: He had a Simpsons cartoon on the wall behind his back!

This client of mine provided the following observation that I want to share with all of you:

"When analyzing video interviews, I realize that most of us do not consider things that we believe to be of less value/importance. Still, most of the time, the interviewer sees these gaps as unforgivable. Executives often work merrily on the content, forgetting the surroundings, the backgrounds, and the outfit. Even after two years of working from home, we still visualize an interview as meeting someone somewhere other than our own home.

Unfortunately, this is not the case in almost all cases, and we must prepare to take care of all counts. Many of us have lost the taste of setting up where we meet people, which used to be our office or conference room, but today is our own home. We have also forgotten that dressing up can help the interlocutors perceive us at first glance.

These are all things that could be useless to us today, but sometimes they do not go unnoticed by the interviewer.

During an interview, I presented a business case and ultimately did not consider my background on my screen, which was the lounge of a famous cartoon. Honestly, I did not even notice this because I was concentrated on my presentation, a PowerPoint that would have been on-screen during the interview.

The interviewer later returned, saying they found my presentation impeccable. Still, they did not believe I could be a good fit in their company because of my unprofessional cartoon background, which they found to be not in line with its culture.

In the beginning, I was disappointed because, to my eyes, having an excellent presentation should not have been diminished by the fact that I had a cartoon background. Can a background ruin everything?!

But, once I started thinking about it, I agreed it could be because not knowing whom we are talking to can make us question if he is a professional or a buffoon. Not everyone accepts jokes during business meetings. This brings us at a crossroads, either be in line with the company's culture or decide to move on and find something more suitable for us in life."

What was the consequence of this interview outcome? This rejection made him change his background setting. He chose a digital background to replace the Simpsons cartoon in the background. Look at the digital background he chose and judge for yourself the difference in perception caused by the new background over the Simpsons one.

Although you're speaking with the same candidate, you will have a totally different perception. I dare to say that many of you ruin interview chances in video interviews because you do not sufficiently prepare for it. The video interview is in a certain sense more challenging since you are the orchestrator of the background and have the ultimate responsibility for it.

#2: OPTIMAL LIGHTING

Irrespective of the light source you choose, you need to make sure you're facing the source. Check the influence of daylight or the absence of it on your face.

For example, you can combine the use of sun blinds with an LED light positioned above your computer screen in the middle of it. See the photo below. If the sun is shining, you risk one half of your face looking bright and the other dark. To create an equally lit face, use the LED light source. In case you want to eliminate the effect of external daylight, you can use the sun blinds to shut it out to a large extent.

Photo by Diethard Kaiserseder – Printed with permission

At all costs, avoid backlighting. Backlighting is the light source behind you.

It casts your shadows forward, making your face look dark and hard to read.

Be smart and work with your surroundings.

Here is an example of a background which is not properly lit at all because of the lack of a natural light source before dawn. In this early morning call, there is not enough daylight, hence the background is pitch black. It's not a good feeling for the interviewer to stare for 30 minutes or longer against a black wall.

Fix your lighting problems because it literally makes you shine or not shine.

One final point: Make sure your glasses don't reflect sun light or artificial light during the interview.

Whether it is artificial light or natural light, light reflecting on the surface of your lenses is irritating and makes you not look good. It ruins the "show," your "show." Unless you have an anti-glare coating for your glasses, then you need to check this before your video interview.

You've probably heard how eye contact and eye movement constitute an important element of non-verbal communication. You will lose that as well if there is a severe glare on your lenses. Watch out especially for sun light entering your room during different stages of the day or sun light reflecting strongly on the windows opposite of you and thereby entering into your work sphere.

To get your lighting equally balanced on either side of the face, often one LED source is not enough. I recommend two LED video light panels with adjustable heights positioned on either side of your desk. A keyword search on e-commerce sites with "video LED lights" will lead you to a selection of products to choose from.

Video savvy Executives and leaders worth mentioning in this context are Satya Nadella, CEO of Microsoft, Nicholas Thompson, CEO at The Atlantic, Brene Brown, CEO/professor/author, Susan Wojcicki, CEO at YouTube, and Melinda and Bill Gates, Co-chairs of the Bill & Melinda Gates Foundation.

No one in 2022, however, has had such a meteoric rise owing to the intensive use of video as Volodymyr Zelenskyy. His formal speeches appear in accord with institutional standards. Zelenskyy appears well framed, with a neutral angle, and illuminated by spotlights, in a classic political scenario where political symbols usually appear. He took the role of political statesman with institutional staging from Kiyev to the world and gained fame, respect, and power in the shortest amount of time after the outbreak of the Russian invasion of Ukraine.

CASE: Ukranian President Volodymyr Zelensky's Speech

President Volodymyr Zelensky's address to the Russians before the country's invasion of Ukraine on February 22, 2022

In the 9-minute video, which got over 1.4 million views, Zelensky passionately addresses the Russians, pleading with them to prevail on their leadership to stop the planned invasion on his country. The speech is rendered in Russian, to show that he directly speaks at and to the Russians.

STAGE SETUP
Zelensky, in a dark suit, stands off-center in front of the flag of Ukraine, the flag of the President of Ukraine, and the map of Ukraine to show the country he represents. The map is made out-of-focus to shift the attention from it and make the President the prominent focus. President Zelensky stands tall with his hands placed by his sides while he keeps a constant look at the camera to show that he's looking into the eyes of the audience. This is not a regular presidential broadcast where the President stands behind a podium.

AUTHENTICITY

Since the Ukrainian leader finds himself in a dire situation, it is expected that he should wear a gloomy look on his face, which he did. Even from his rasping voice, one would quickly discover that he isn't at ease and has possibly been overstretched. The passionate way through which he delivers the speech and the facts he gives to support his claim make him likable, relatable, and authentic. As a leader that he is, he is unafraid to show how distressed his country's situation is.

PASSION

Zelensky speaks with great conviction. His knowledge of history allows him to allude to well-known events and places to show that he knows his audience well and shares certain experiences with them. To show that he has been wrongly portrayed, he recounts how his grandfather fought as a Soviet soldier but died in an independent Ukraine. In a bid to make his points known, he brilliantly poses compelling questions to his audience and immediately answers them.

CONFIDENCE

Though Zelensky appears battered, he stands firm and resolute for his people. This is depicted in how he shows his readiness to defend his people if Russia ends up launching an attack on Ukraine. He further demonstrates how his country's resistance would be resolute. This shows that he stands with and pursues whatever he believes in.

IMPACT

Zelensky didn't rush through his speech. He carefully explains his points and observes several pauses to give the audience enough time to process whatever he has said. The aim of the speech is to bring a larger portion of Russians—if not all—to his side by appealing to their emotions, and he keeps the focus of the message on the negative effect of the atrocities Russia was committing. This will ultimately make the audience join voices with those of the international community in condemning the planned invasion (as at then).

Video link: https://www.youtube.com/watch?v=Fwzb_JX7u04

#3: USING NOTES DISCREETLY AND EFFECTIVELY

As an executive, you are probably accustomed to reading from notes during a presentation and taking notes during important meetings and conversations. But, you might be asking, how do these actions affect your Hollywood Setting during a video interview in the Hidden Job Market?

Unfortunately, the answer isn't black and white, but there are a few things you can keep in mind and tricks you can have up your sleeve. Let's discuss.

READING FROM NOTES DURING A VIDEO INTERVIEW

The question of whether or not it is appropriate to read from notes during an interview is a highly debatable one. Interviews are considered a form of business meeting where proposals are being made and ideas are reeled out. Since it's a video interview and not a physical one, the interviewer may not be able to see everything you have on your desk.

That being said, you definitely can have notes during your interview if it makes you feel more confident and sound like you have more expertise. But, you should do so as discreetly as possible because you want to avoid distracting your interviewer at all costs.

The power of distraction is a powerful one, as we've previously discussed. The interviewer can quickly and easily become distracted, causing them to miss important insights you may be sharing. This is a serious threat— one that could even cost you the opportunity if you aren't careful.

There are two tricks I have seen.

Number one: What if you absolutely want to remind yourself of some keywords? What can you do? In the case where you have your web camera or built-in camera positioned correctly, which is slightly above your head, positioning a post-it with a keyword or keywords maybe a safe option to remain unnoticed.

Number two: You write on a whiteboard or paper and stick it against the wall to read from.

> **Avoid letting your eyes "walk" away slightly from focus on your interviewer to read from your notes, screen post-its, or the wall behind it.**

Rheinmetal AG executive Boris Maiweg laughs about these types of manipulations. He warns executives that interviewers can sense when you are digressing even a little with your attention or eye contact and comments: "Those folks are usually a no-go."

My personal advice is not to read from notes. Try to avoid it. Put extra energy in your interview preparation to overcome "stage fright." Notes are taking a heavy toll on your confidence and attention, and they prevent you from being fully present. You always think, "I better read my notes before I forget something" and actually do it. And the interviewer is likely to spot this anomaly in one way or another which creates an uncomfortable feeling or a less-than-optimal impression.

Furthermore, using notes might lead you to make your responses too long. Keep it short—ideally two minutes or less. When you get to the point, you are combating the power of distraction and helping your interviewer stay focused, engaged, and interested.

Those of you who heavily rely on scripting or reading aids during interviews should read my book *Peak Performance Interviewing for Executives* to learn more about effective interview techniques which do not require notes of any kind.

TAKING NOTES DURING A VIDEO INTERVIEW

Note taking is a sign for the interviewer that you take their information seriously. You may decide to use the opportunity to write down key details that can help you formulate answers to subsequent interviews. If you're the type that gets nervous and easily forgets things of significant importance, then taking notes can help you to combat the challenge to ensure you do not miss out on any point during the process of responding to a question.

Notes are also useful at the end of the interview when the interview asks if you have any questions for them. As an interviewer, I believe that an interviewee with a prepared list of questions, for instance, is more intentional than someone without any. Therefore, the notes you took during the interview can be a good source for formulating possible questions.

Nevertheless, you need to maintain great caution while taking notes, especially if you place them too low on your desk. This is because the moment your eyes start wandering away from the camera in successions or you bury your head in your notepad, you're showing a form of disconnection which can be off-putting to the interviewer.

I repeat my warning: Be careful when taking notes. To observe what you appear like "on the other side" from the perspective of the interviewer, practice taking notes in front of a camera with a partner. The majority of people, including myself, have a tendency to lean forward and look at their notepad. This means that your interviewer will now only be able to see the top of your head, which may show your bald scalp if you are a man—not what you want them to notice from an aesthetic standpoint. Unaware of it, you make a fool of yourself.

You are also setting your interviewer up to become distracted and disengaged from the interview, which means they could miss valuable information you are sharing about yourself. Again, don't let the power of distraction cost you an opportunity.

Also, irrespective of how you place your notes, they only serve as a written aid and not a script. Therefore, they shouldn't lead the discussion or make you derail the conversation. The most important thing is to keep your notes organized, avoid distraction, make a connection, and keep the flow of the conversation as smooth as possible.

AI Notetaker by Fathom is an app that makes it **easy to recall and share important moments** from your Zoom meetings. Instead of hurriedly taking notes, you are able to **focus on the conversation** and get the most out of your meetings.

BENEFITS OF USING THE AI NOTETAKER INCLUDE:
- Get recordings, transcription, and summaries of key moments of the call so you don't miss a beat
- Send out your post-call follow-ups, as recordings are available instantly once your call ends
- Share meeting highlights with colleagues for easy review (because no one wants to rewatch a meeting)

As a Zoom One subscriber, you get premium access to this app so that it will be part of your Zoom meeting experience.

CHAPTER 4 CHEAT SHEET
VIDEO INTERVIEW SETTING

This is a list of action items to improve your video interview setting for optimal video interview performance.

DOWNLOAD THE CHEAT SHEET

ON VIDEO INTERVIEW SETTING HERE:

www.hiddenexecutivejobs.com/video-interviews

"May the Force be with you is charming but it's not important. What's important is that you become the Force – for yourself and perhaps for other people."
—Harrison Ford

Perception is reality. And that's what makes interviewing so difficult. Yet, the art of interviewing is easier if you bear in mind that in this New World of Digital Engagement, 90% of success is how you come across and only 10% is verbal. Most people focus on the 10% verbal. We all know those interview books talking about the 10, 20, or 100 most important interview questions and answers, resulting in memorizing scripted answers and failure in interviews. My two other interviewing books *Peak Performance Interviewing for Executives* and *Perfect Pitching for Executives in the Hidden Job Market* together cover this 10% verbal in detail. Let us discuss in this chapter the other vital 90%.

Before we do that, you need to understand the power of bias in shaping the 90%.

VIDEO INTERVIEW BIAS: COGNITIVE BIAS

Usually, the video interview is an avenue for executive candidates to reveal their intangible qualities to interviewers. However, you need to realize that interviewers are humans and, therefore, are not immune to misjudgment. By this, I mean that interviewers may be faced with certain biases that impact their decisions. Such biases may relate to how quickly or slowly candidates have approached the first question.

Let's quickly examine a few cognitive biases that may determine how an interviewer perceives an interviewee.

THE IKEA EFFECT

Simply put, the IKEA effect describes how people tend to like, love, or value the things they create. In the case of a video interview, candidates feel more valued when they create an impact out of their own efforts. Therefore, when you are interviewing for a position, the IKEA effect can motivate you to feel more engaged and committed to the process.

On the flipside, the IKEA effect might make interviewers increase the value they place on their culture, so organizations often seek candidates that fit into their culture. Therefore, you would have to 'work' with the interviewers to prove whether or not you're fit for the position you're interviewing for.

BANDWAGON EFFECT

This is the probability of an interviewer adopting a belief based on the number of people holding that belief. Consider it as a form of groupthink. Often, when you have a group of interviewers with a majority of them expressing similar views, the rest may feel reluctant to share a different view, thus leading them to become subjective, biased opinions which ultimately lead to poor judgments.

THE HALO EFFECT

This is a bias where the first impression an interviewer has about a candidate has a spillover effect on their other traits. In other words, if based on the initial part of the conversation, an interviewer perceives a candidate to be competent in an area, then they assume they have the same level of competency in other areas.

The reason is simple. They simply see what they want, or expect to see. During the hiring process, this assumption may cause interviewers to miss out on a key evaluation point of an executive candidate—good or bad.

Interviewer bias makes it even harder to understand interviews and decisions about your interview performance.

> *"Perception is reality. In this New World of Digital Engagement 90% is how you come across, 10% is verbal."*
> —Rainer Maria Morita

NON-VERBAL COMMUNICATION DURING VIDEO INTERVIEWS

Most times, interviewers forget almost all the things you said during an interview conversation, but what they remember easily is the impression you made. In fact, the notion that conversation is 10% verbal and 90% nonverbal relies on an analysis of the theory of Albert Mehrabian. It reveals that face-to-face communication is 55% nonverbal, 38% vocal, and 7% words. Either way, the fact remains that interviewers look beyond verbal communication.

On a movie set, directors, producers, camera operators, and other experts often line up verbal communication with nonverbal cues. Even actors could have written notes for nonverbal cues that do not appear in the script but will help to enhance the dialogue.

When you join a video interview call, even before speaking, your body language, your facial expressions, your voice pitch and tone, and all other aspects of paralanguage already reveal your level of confidence and professionalism, even without saying a word. This is to show that nonverbal communication contributes to how your interviewers perceive and learn more about you.

As a Morita Method Executive, you need to familiarize yourself with non-verbal communication cues that underline a video interview process to

- Deliver messages with the desired maximum impact
- Engage with decisionmakers, build rapport, and make them open up to you

Let's quickly dive into the most important nonverbal cues.

#1: MAINTAIN GOOD BODY POSTURE

Posture constitutes an important aspect of acting. When actors maintain excellent postures, they are able to easily move as well as project their voice with more power. As a rule of thumb in maintaining good body posture in a video interview, you need to be at an arm's length from your screen.

You don't want to get too close to the screen that your interviewers get put off by any of your body parts. Crossing your arms, slouching, falling back, or sinking into your chair, for instance, can make you appear as less confident, too casual, and uninterested in the process.

Good body posture means maintaining a straight back with your chest out, your arms to the side, and your feet planted firmly on the ground. This sends a signal that you are positioned in a way that reflects confidence.

However, you should not be too static either. If you overdo it and are too stiff, you risk coming across as awkward and boring.

To signal "listening mode" to the interviewer, tilt your head slightly and maintain an open posture. Do not cross your arms, or your counterpart may feel less inclined to share information.

The best is to get others involved. Get their feedback on your image and video performance.

#2: MAINTAIN EYE CONTACT

The second rule of successful non-verbal communication is to maintain comfortable eye contact. Eye contact is important for building rapport. In a face to face setting, you simply keep eye contact without trying. It is as simple as that.

In video interviews, though, you need to look straight into the web camera and not at the interviewer on your screen. To create a digital executive presence, you simply have to look into your camera rather than your screen. By so doing, an impression that you are looking into the eyes of the person(s) on the other side of the call is created, and this can signal an emotional connection.

It is important to keep eye contact in a way that feels comfortable. You don't want to keep too much eye contact. In other words, good eye contact doesn't have to involve staring into your interviewer's eyes intently. Rather, it follows a natural flow.

You would think that everybody naturally keeps focus on the screen or better the camera.

Unfortunately, this is not the case. I know CEOs and CxOs who have bad habits such as looking away. Look at the cases below. The executives are excessively looking upwards while talking. What impression does it make on you?

Look into your web camera and not the screen of your device.

#3: MAINTAIN AN APPROPRIATE TONE OF VOICE

Your voice should contribute to creating a positive first and lasting winning impression.

Video communication requires more attention to your voice than face-to-face communication. Video lowers or changes the impact of your voice in an adverse manner creating immediate negative impressions on the interviewer's side.

Don't get too preoccupied with how you dress that you neglect how you sound. Here is the thing: the way you sound conveys a lot to the interviewer. Most times, **it is not what you say that matters.** Rather, it is actually **how you say it**.

For professional actors, voice is an important tool that helps to add nuances. It is for this reason that they work hard to strengthen their voice. This, of course, takes another level of training.

Due to the fact that your voice shapes words, giving them different feelings and meanings when spoken, interviewers are quick to tell who you are from your tone. For instance, a monotonous, low-pitch voice simply sends a signal that you're timid and not interested in the interview process.

The reality is that your interviewers do not want the same voice pitch throughout an interview process. Therefore, identify parts of the conversations where you should mind your pace, take a pause, or maintain an emphasis. For instance, you may want to speed up your tone of voice if you want to show interest in a certain part of the process.

In all, it is important that you project your voice and maintain clarity. This demonstrates good communication.

#4: SMILE GENUINELY

Smile. The fastest way to create a connection between yourself and someone else is to smile at them. Smiling is the fastest way you can improve your body language performance. But smile genuinely because decisionmakers can spot a fake smile easily.

That being said, however, you need to consider the cultural context in which you're having the conversation. Smiling means different things in different cultures. Americans, Australians, and Canadians smile to express happiness and tell the other person that they're people they can talk to. However, in cultures such as Russia or Japan, you should stay away from smiling during video interviews.

While you can hide your legs during a video interview, your face will never leave the camera. This is why you should not focus on what you say alone but rather focus on your facial expressions when saying it. When you are not smiling, you are simply projecting a lack of excitement, passion, joy, and friendliness, which is usually a turnoff for interviewers

The fact that you want to appear serious during a video interview doesn't mean you shouldn't smile, especially when your interviewer says something funny. Apart from projecting friendliness, smiling also sends signals of warmth, energy, and enthusiasm to interviewers.

Show your smile. Don't overdo it, though. With moderation, it is perfect.

Let's look at the three photos below.

The first photo shows an executive with a timid expression. No smile. Overall, this creates a negative interview impression.

The second photo shows the same executive looking slightly worried but otherwise with an indifferent or neutral expression. Overall, an "Okayish" impression but far away from impressing your counterpart. It doesn't feel like he's being genuine, which makes him harder to trust.

In the third photo, the same executive has a natural, joyful smile and a positively beaming facial aura. This is the winning smile you want for yourself.

#5: NOD APPROPRIATELY

A video interview is basically a conversation between you and another person on the other side of the call. While you're being engaged during the process, you want to connect with what your interviewer is saying to let them know you're getting along with them. You might be tempted to continue nodding uncontrollably. This sends a bad signal to the interviewers.

Of course, you want to create the impression that you are listening intently as you're being engaged. However, you should avoid too much nodding and keep your motion in check. Otherwise, you will create the impression that you're getting tired of the conversation. Pick the right spots where nodding naturally aligns with the conversation and don't overdo it.

#6: DRESS PROFESSIONALLY

Whether or not you've got passion for fashion, your appearance says much about your level of confidence. Professional actors are advised to appear in an outfit that is comfortable and fits the role for which they are auditioning. Through that, their personalities get revealed and their best features are highlighted.

Just because you're interviewing from the comfort of your home doesn't mean you can simply show up as you wish. For instance, you don't want to interview for an executive position in an organization with a conservative culture while wearing an unbuttoned shirt, exposing your hairy body and heavy use of accessories. In fact, you'd be disqualified even without having your competency tested.

A neat, well-groomed appearance can show that you are committed to the position. Since you're interviewing over video, it is recommended that you opt for a plain shirt or a shirt with less patterns, neatly ironed. Also, dress up your bottom half so you don't get caught out in your pajamas if you need to stand up. You may also want to minimize accessories, so your interviewers don't get distracted by them.

Above all, what you wear should align with the company culture. You may have to get some clues about how you'd be expected to appear at work from the company website.

#7: WEAR THE RIGHT GLASSES

Glasses matter because your identity matters. Glasses are a powerful way to express or underline your personality and one of the most striking accessories impacting the perception others have of us. The good news is that manufacturers of glasses and opticians offer a seemingly endless choice of models to cater to the needs of anyone.

Executives often do not pay enough attention to glasses. The wrong glasses create the wrong impression on others or create a weak impact. This happens more often to men than to women. Women, in general, pay more attention to how they look than men. In general, it is better to wear no glasses than to wear the wrong glasses.

#8 MIRROR THE INTERVIEWER

This simply means copying his or her behaviour. When the interviewer leans forward and starts to whisper with smiles, you should slowly do the same. When the interviewer laughs, you should offer a chuckle as well. Mirroring is a non-verbal technique to show empathy and interest. Good listeners intuitively mimic another person's body language and vocal qualities because it builds rapport and can increase attraction.

——————— CASE: Mirror the CEO ———————

This is a real-world case of a CFO interview with the CEO of a highly respected industry association. My role was to effectively prepare my candidate for the CFO interview. He was eager to share his goals, plans, and strategy for increasing the association's revenue with the CEO during the interview.

I instructed my candidate to let go of his entire interview preparation. I suggested that he use "active listening" as a successful interview technique.

I learned that the CEO was very conservative. I also discovered that he valued applicants who were happy to listen, take direction, and carry it out.

I therefore advised my candidate to let the CEO own the room and run his "CEO show." I advised him to be passive during the interview, listen extra carefully, and, on top of that, mirror him by emulating his behaviour.

In retrospect, the one tactic that worked with this CEO was to be quiet, a good listener, and to mirror.

> **I cannot overemphasize that interviews are always case by case.**

RECORD YOURSELF

If you aren't confident in your nonverbal cues, then recording yourself on your computer or mobile device is the quickest approach to evaluate your own performance. You won't receive the same feedback as you would from an interview coach or executive career advisor like myself nor is this method equivalent to recommendations from people you know. However, because you can see and hear yourself as other people would on your phone or computer screen, you may gradually improve your video performance and technological setup this way.

LEARNING MY OWN LESSONS

One of my clients was having a really hard time getting the proper message across. An experienced CEO admitted to him that instead of appearing as an advisor, he gave off the vibe of a TV news anchor because of how his upper body took up too much of the screen. He was also completely still and stationary throughout the video, and his speech pattern was similar to that of a telegram reporter. This feedback enabled him to adjust his video appearance to be more advisor-like.

With this new set up, he is positioned chest up and looks more relaxed. No necktie is worn. You can see that his left hand is holding his head, and his fingers are pointing at his brain. This movement is connected to thinking and assessing what is being said. By using body language like that, he gets a little bit closer to capturing the true essence of an advisor, whose job it is to frequently and critically review their customers' points of view.

Perception is reality. Get others involved. Get their feedback on your image and video performance.

CHAPTER 5 CHEAT SHEET
VIDEO INTERVIEW PERFORMANCE

This is a list of action items to optimize your interview performance in video interviews.

DOWNLOAD THE CHEAT SHEET

ON VIDEO INTERVIEW

PERFORMANCE HERE:

www.hiddenexecutivejobs.com/video-interviews

CHAPTER 6: AUTHENTICITY

"Don't trade authenticity for approval."
—Leslie Cassidy

When auditioning for a movie role, actors are encouraged to convey their authentic selves, especially through their interactions and gestures. Rather than showing up as a series of personas, thereby presenting different faces, a good way to get connected to the audience is by showing the real person behind the personas, with absolutely nothing to hide. Only authentic actors can make a real difference.

As an executive interviewee, your chances of success depend partly on how well you answer questions posed to you and, most importantly, how well you present yourself. Since video interviews are a form of real conversation, interviewers want to engage with the real you. Displaying your authenticity starts by considering your interests and passion and staying with them even when others consider them unacceptable.

Many interviewees, more often than not, try to show off and sweep interviewers off their feet by impressing them with what they consider as "perfect" answers or appearance even when they know they're being economical with the truth or wearing a fake look. This is a great mistake. Let me tell you this: Interviews are a means of exploring how a relationship can be mutually beneficial. And such a relationship must be built on trust even if it means you have to become vulnerable.

Besides, when you try to be something else, you may find it difficult to keep up with it. In fact, your true self will reveal itself through other means—take, for instance, through other things you say. Of course, you'd be jeopardizing your chances to take on the job or perform up to par when you eventually get employed.

That being said, you should not always consider what you feel the interviewers want to hear from you but be more interested in showing what they should know about you. Despite the fact that you want to appear as professional as possible, you should also make sure your real YOU comes through during the process. No one wants to work with someone whose authenticity meter is on the low.

Rather than trick the interviewers into believing that you're one thing when, in reality, you're another thing, present yourself in a way that accurately represents your beliefs, interests, values, and passions. However, by so doing, you need to maintain the right balance between revealing your real self and demonstrating how your personality fits into the role for which you're interviewing.

Let's quickly get into four aspects that can help you appear as authentic as possible: purpose, vision, looks, and setting.

PURPOSE

Understanding and articulating your purpose can give you a significant edge, especially when interviewing for purpose-driven companies. Brands like Patagonia, Tetra Pak, Tesla, Quicksilver, Red Bull, and Harley Davidson prioritize individuals who align with their core values.

Being authentic in a video interview entails acting in harmony with your true self. It's not just about presenting a rehearsed persona; it's about revealing who you genuinely are. What this means is that your purpose or why should be closely tied to the identity of your real self. This involves:

1. **Understanding Your Core**: Recognize your values, beliefs, and motivations. Knowing your "why" provides clarity, and when shared honestly, resonates with others.

2. **Avoiding Inauthenticity**: Trying to be someone you're not to gain approval often results in a disjointed identity presentation. Authenticity is key to truly connecting with your audience.

3. **Reflective Questions**: To discern your purpose, ponder:
   - What drives me?
   - Why have I chosen this path?
   - What are the emotions behind my decisions?
   - What do I stand for?

If you forcefully live a life that consistently seeks the approval of others, as opposed to what serves your authenticity, then you'll always come off as hiding a certain part of your identity. And you cannot find your purpose when you stay inauthentic.

In fact, you will be unable to convey the right message about your personality when you don't know what you stand for—that is, your purpose. By articulating your why, you'll be able to determine your value proposition, which is the unique blend of qualities and motivations you bring to the table which sets you apart from others. Clearly conveying this can create a powerful connection with your interviewers, fostering trust in both your character and capabilities.

Remember, it's not about fitting a mold or meeting others' expectations. Embrace and express your true self. When you do, the right opportunities and connections will follow.

VISION

Discovering your why serves as a pathway towards expressing yourself. Over the years, I have seen interviewees paint a supercilious vision when they were asked where they see themselves in the future. For instance, it is common to hear some of them say they see themselves becoming a director, for instance. While it's good to have a vision, most interviewees bloat that vision, which often turns out to be too illusory and, therefore, not genuine.

This is not to say that you should not have an idea of where you want to be in the future. In fact, having knowledge of your vision helps you stay in touch with it. However, the moment you try to be another copy of a boss or personality you admire, you may be less likely to be perceived as real.

Therefore, having knowledge of who you really are will help direct you and make you stay true to your vision. This, however, requires that you pay attention to your inner thoughts and the way you respond to the external world.

Rather than force yourself to fit into a role, a better approach would be to describe the features of the kind of role you'd desire in the future. This way, you'd have represented the only—and, of course, true—version of yourself. For instance, if you're the kind of person that loves a creative industry, you may find a job that requires a lot of formalities to be draining. Instead, you'd probably want a work where work activities will not take away from or diminish your personal persona.

LOOKS

You only get one chance to create a winning positive impression. And your looks play a major role in this.

ADVICE FOR FEMALE EXECUTIVES

Your looks should be colorful yet classic at the same time. The photo below is a good example of colorful yet classic looks.

Source: Franziska Schneebeli, Printed with permission

Communication and change management expert Franziska Schneebeli gives female executives the following guidelines for how to dress:

"Dress in a simple, yet elegant way, adapted to the respective industry. Bring in colour in line with your personality, your main messages and with the surroundings (background, location, etc.). It should also match the culture of the organization and their country of origin.

I recommend glasses for online interviews only in top lighting, otherwise contact lenses are the better option.

Discreet jewellery is a nice accessory and "refines" the impression.

Put on a little more make-up than usual in front of the camera."

ADVICE FOR MALE EXECUTIVES

"Shall I wear a suit and necktie?" is a question that my clients often ask me. The general advice is, as always, case by case.

It depends very much on the interviewer, the role you are interviewing for, the industry and culture of the company, and the culture of the country in which the company is operating in.

The finance industry in general is conservative, while fintech or crypto industries are less formal. So, wear a suit and necktie for financial industry interviews and smart casual for fintech or crypto industry interviews. If you interview for membership organizations which have a rather conservative client membership body, such as the Association of the Automobile Industry, the International Air Transport Association, or the banking industry association, then your looks should reflect it.

In recent years all around the globe, I've noticed that wearing a suit and necktie, especially during hot summer months, is no longer expected. Instead, wearing a decent business shirt without a necktie or a business shirt with a jacket has become widely accepted.

ADVICE FOR MALE AND FEMALE EXECUTIVES

"Clothes make people" is an old saying true for many interviews. Dress for success and authenticity but also in a way that makes you feel comfortable. Would you hire yourself the way you look? Do you believe in the image you have about yourself and the way you dress? Does your outfit and general appearance make you feel good? If so, go for it. Otherwise, fix the issues.

> **Dress as if you were at work. Imagine being with your clients, showing the best version of yourself up to every detail, including business footwear, and make sure you are comfortable under the skin.**

A common mistake most interviewees make is that they want to adapt to the company they're applying for. Sometimes, this might make you appear in a manner that is unreflective of who you really are, thus leaving the interviewers with the wrong impression about your priorities, interests, and values. I call such people clowns because they try to please the interviewer during the interview with less consideration for themselves. Don't compromise on what is important for you and how you want to show up. Don't be a clown; be a beacon of your career and job search goals and vision.

——— CASE: McKinsey Image Trap ———

While graduates and junior professionals try desperately to get into this prestigious consultancy called McKinsey, some senior consulting industry executives have a terrible time losing their consulting industry image. Their typical McKinsey looks stay with them even years after they have left the company without realizing it.

One executive who used to work for McKinsey several years ago and is now head of strategy in a medical device company could not understand why headhunters always offered him consulting jobs either in the consulting industry or internal consulting in large companies although he stated that he wanted to become general manager. I immediately understood the reason. He looked like a perfect McKinsey consultant—classic dark suit with white shirt and classic necktie. The same "McKinsey" type photos spread as profile photos in social media and on his resume. He had outgrown his "McKinsey" consulting industry looks a long time ago but was unaware of his need to change it to advance in his career.

If you think you may have fallen into an image "trap" like this, then talk to your coach or other experts in this field because it may be time for an image makeover.

SETTING

What comes to the minds of your interviewers immediately when they see your background? Does it reflect who you are? Or do you leave interviewers confused about what you represent, thus diminishing trust? Do you know you can leverage your setting as a subtle way to tell interviewers something about yourself?

Many interviewees, in a bid to impress the interviewers, go as far as creating a room setting or digital background that less suits their personality. Remember, you have total control over a video interview setting, so why not use it to your advantage then? By using a setting that helps interviewers learn about you, you'll come off as more authentic.

A good reference point is how Hollywood stars get professional when selecting settings for a movie. They are aware of how setting helps the audience to come to terms with the actions and background of the characters in the story. Therefore, the settings they use convey various important messages.

As an executive interviewee that seeks to be like Hollywood stars, you can take a cue from the following possible settings.

When talking to Swiss clients or those related to Switzerland, I often use the aerial view of Lausanne with Lake Geneva and a snow-capped mountain range to convey the image of a traditional Swiss town embedded in a natural setting of mesmerizing beauty suggesting the stale Swiss economic conditions with high quality of life.

People wonder, "Why Lausanne?" since German-speaking Zurich is the more obvious choice. I choose Lausanne over Zurich because it strongly resonates with my values, beliefs, and lifestyle: international, culture-rich, a long-standing vine tradition, advanced science and research ground, unifying the world through the spirit of sports, and offering a fantastic blend of sports and leisure possibilities through all seasons.

When discussing software, chip, or high-tech opportunities, I often use the Golden Gate Bridge during sunrise as a symbol of the power and progress of the United States. I also like the image of a bridge because it fits my image of a solution provider or bridge-builder in the Hidden Job Market.

In the aspects of automotive opportunities in Germany, I usually select Munich because it is an automotive hub that has an impressive aerial view surrounded by mountains representing a traditional German city with good quality of life that I know well.

In short, a professional background with a view conveys a professional and accomplished impression; a board meeting room gives you a C-suite touch and creates a peer in the board room atmosphere for your interview conversation; and a fine art background can reinforce your message using the power and sublime nature of artworks.

JUST BE YOURSELF

Being just the way you are is the simplest route to authenticity. There is no technology, no Hollywood setting, and no peak performance interview methodology that can make you authentic if you are not yourself. I see executives struggling a lot in this respect. And the reasons are obvious. Most executives work without passion. I mean that what they are passionate about is not the object of their work. A research study revealed 85% of executives are disconnected from their passion.

I can give you countless examples of executives or so-called experts in the business world who are successful businessman but without passion for their business. I am privileged to have amazingly talented leaders as my coaching clients who are ready to build a passionate career towards their highest dreams instead of continuing to be fake. The professional service industry is full of fake people.

Let us take consulting. The consulting industry attracts highly talented people who like consulting, but the more you advance to the top ranks, the more you are pushed to achieve sales quota. Some call it the "rat race." It is all about money. Not to mention the many consulting executives who are apathetic about consulting and do the rat race for years, if not decades, although they secretly yearn to do something else.

There is the $1M consulting industry CEO who is passionate about river rafting.

There is the $300K finance industry CFO who has a passion for equipping average Africans on the street with basic financial wealth management tools.

There is the $400K insurance industry CFO who is passionate about sports—in particular outdoor sports.

There is the $250K analog design architect who is refurbishing old motorcycles again and again.

There is the $250K HR Executive from the coffee beverage industry who is passionate about art and creating her own art.

There is the $400K B2B industrial CEO who is wildly passionate about guitar playing and performing as lead vocal in a band.

There is the $300K strategy consulting industry MD who is passionate about making high quality textile and apparel products.

There is the $400K finance industry manageress who is passionate about vintage bags for ladies.

There is the $500K industrial IoT executive who is passionate about having his own business.

There is the $400K electric utility CEO whose childhood dream was aerospace, who studied aerospace, who became an award winning aerospace researcher and project manager and then "got stuck" in electric utilities.

There is the $250K software sales directrice who is passionate about music therapy, studied music therapy, and healed handicapped children with music therapy but remains in software "because of the money."

John Lennon said: "Life is what happens when you are busy with other projects."

I can only give Akira Morita, the founder of Sony, Soichiro Honda, the founder of Honda Motors, Alain Ducasse, the French gourmet chef-de-cuisine and gourmet entrepreneur, or Richard Branson as few among countless examples of authenticity. Ordinary people create extraordinary things.

What are your secret passion projects that you do in your free time or during holidays?

> **Don't pretend to be someone else. Don't be fake. Your authenticity drops dramatically or you lose it entirely.**

Changing direction or building a passionate career when you are a highly paid executive is a very challenging undertaking. As a first step and for a more detailed discussion, read my book *Find Your Career Passion. Towards Abundant Joy, Fulfillment and Authenticity in Your Job, Career and Life.*

WHAT'S YOUR MESSAGE?

What is your main message in interviews? A lot of executives do not have a main message. Is this message truly YOU? When asked about vision, mission, and value, are you true to yourself or bending to the needs of the hiring company?

I remember a Chief Sustainability Officer client of mine. Together, we worked out that he stands for ethical leadership in a world where top management practices greenwashing. One example of greenwashing is when a company runs multimillion-dollar advertising campaigns that portray highly polluting energy companies as eco-friendly.

This Chief Sustainability Officer commented on his choices as follows:

"I also think it truly reflects who I am, and what I genuinely believe in. And therefore I am also in agreement with you: that focus may deter some potential employers indeed, but then it means these are not the ones I would be happy working with. I think this focus on "ethical leadership" may close a few doors, but it will open the right ones."

To what extent do you know yourself? People who do not know themselves will have a difficult time leading others. People who do not know themselves are likely to have issues presenting themselves and their candidature in a compelling way.

The period between 2003 and 2020 represented a steady growth period where it was enough for leaders to deliver expected results. With the advent of the COVID crisis and the transition to the new normal, companies realized that they needed leaders with strong soft skills, able to lead people in a brittle, anxious, non-linear, and incomprehensible world. In the new normal, companies heavily screen for leaders who know themselves and their values and who take a stance. Better to take a stance and err, rather than take no stance and be screened out as a "nobody" for lack of leadership.

When Piyush Gupta took office as CEO of DBS Bank in Singapore in 2009, he released clear messages about the direction of the company, one of which was: "I will manage DBS as if it was a software company." For example, he complained about how too much bureaucracy and time is needed to open a bank account. He no longer wanted customers to queue in the bank premises and take one hour or more to open a bank account. Today, it will take just five minutes to get your bank account.

Look where Piyush Gupta took DBS up to the present. DBS is a leading financial services group in Asia with a presence in 18 markets.

Headquartered and listed in Singapore, DBS has a growing presence in the three key Asian axes of growth: Greater China, Southeast Asia, and South Asia. The bank's capital position, as well as "AA-" and "Aa1" credit ratings, is among the highest in Asia-Pacific. DBS has been recognised for its global leadership, having been named "World's Best Bank" by Euromoney, "Global Bank of the Year" by The Banker, and "Best Bank in the World" by Global Finance. DBS has also been at the forefront of shaping the future of banking, having been recognised as "World's Best Digital Bank" by Euromoney twice. In addition, DBS has been accorded the "Safest Bank in Asia" award by Global Finance for 13 consecutive years from 2009 to 2021.

──── CASE: Authenticity ────

Being authentic in video interviews requires that you say only what you believe is right, even when it puts you at risk of being rejected or condemned. A case study would be the case of Johnson & Johnson being hit by a major disaster—Tylenol cyanide poisoning in the US in 1982. This was totally unexpected for the longstanding medicine as it was intentional, and the CEO James Burke followed his instinct and was authentic in his communication strategy.

> *In the fall of 1982, Johnson & Johnson was enmeshed in a corporate crisis that pushed it close to the end of the cliff. The crisis was the Tylenol poisoning that caused the death of seven persons. Its CEO, James Burke, played a significant role in managing the crisis - which bordered on public trust - and helping the company bounce back to its pre-crisis sales level.*

He was decisive in managing the crisis. He swiftly held a news conference and was ready to appear on interviews at any instance, revealing the true circumstances that led to the ugly situation as well as the actions the company was taking to arrest the situation. Some of the actions included set up of toll-free numbers, sending of 450,000 telex messages to doctors' offices, hospitals and trade groups, recall and destruction of all 31 million bottles of Tylenol capsules on store, and stopping of all Tylenol advertising.

Burke's decision for wholesale recall of Tylenol was met with a fierce resistance from the FBI and FDA. However, he maintained that it was "the right solution, either from the point of view of the public, or from the point of view of his company's business." This cost the company a record loss of over $100 million.

He further led a campaign against the use of Tylenol, encouraging consumers to only buy the product when it was declared safe. His openness and the decisive steps he took were in conformity with the Credo, the summation of corporate values, which he accused the company's top executives of neglecting.

The lessons to be learned from the leadership displayed by Mr Burke revolve around knowing one's values and living by them, being prepared to face crises, and, most importantly, saying the truth no matter how it makes one appear or feel.

CHAPTER 6 CHEAT SHEET
AUTHENTICITY

This is a list of actions to improve your authenticity for optimal video interview performance.

DOWNLOAD THE CHEAT SHEET

ON AUTHENTICITY IN VIDEO

INTERVIEWS HERE:

www.hiddenexecutivejobs.com/video-interviews

CHAPTER 7: PASSION

"A passionate video interview performance —without unnecessary exaggerations and exaltations—is a learned behaviour."
—Rainer Maria Morita

A cting is considered as the ability to convey passion. Therefore, actors are passionate people who love the art of acting so much that they keep practicing to put on an outstanding performance. The audience, in turn, sees the character in them, rather than the actor.

One of the things most interviewers look for in candidates is passion. They believe that passionate interviewees perform well when they get hired for the position for which they're interviewing. This may not be always true, but it definitely draws the interviewer to one's side.

As simple as passion may sound, conveying it during a video interview process is not always an easy ride. This is where it gets tricky. You don't tell passion, you show it. At the same time, you also don't want to sound desperate and less enthusiastic.

How do you then show that you are genuinely interested in the role you're interviewing for? Here are a few strategies to help you communicate your passion during a video interview.

#1: SHARE A COMPELLING PERSONAL STORY
Most of the time, the first question an interviewer tends to ask is this:

"Tell us about yourself." While you may see it as the usual initial question, consider it an opportunity given to you to communicate your passion in a way that leaves a memorable impression with the interviewers. By crafting your skills, education, and experience into a compelling narrative, the interviewers are interested in the conversation.

#2: ASK COMPELLING QUESTIONS

Get this right. The interviewer isn't the only one who gets to ask all the questions; you should always prepare to ask questions too. In fact, interviewers do not consider candidates without any questions as really interested in the position they are interviewing for. Remember, you may be competing against other candidates, and you wouldn't want to slim down your chances of getting hired just because you failed to ask compelling questions. Therefore, asking questions shows you're not only curious but also interested in both the company and role.

#3: BE AUTHENTIC

Sometimes, you don't need to overly highlight your passion and interests. There are ways you can make them shine through your conversation by being genuine and authentic. Even if you can fake a lot of things, especially your job-related experiences, you simply can't fake passion. Be yourself and answer all questions as honestly as possible and steer the interview in a proactive way. Back up your passion with concrete proof points.

#4: SAY HOW PASSIONATE YOU ARE ABOUT THE COMPANY, ITS BRANDS, AND ITS LEADERS

Before deciding to work for a company, you most likely love what they're doing, which has motivated you to want to be a part of them. This could be anything from their work culture to their reputation or even the unique products or services they offer or the leaders they have. Who doesn't love to be complimented?

CHAPTER 7 CHEAT SHEET
PASSION

This is a list of actions to improve your passion for optimal video interview performance.

DOWNLOAD THE CHEAT SHEET

ON PASSION IN VIDEO

INTERVIEWS HERE:

www.hiddenexecutivejobs.com/video-interviews

CONCLUSION

V ideo interview success is a learned behaviour, especially in the Hidden Job Market. The way to the top is clear—rehearse, rehearse, rehearse. Take your video performance from good to better and from better to best, and restart. This athletic attitude seems to be completely missing in the international executive job search arena. Executives are obsessed with their resumes and dedicate substantial efforts and resources to always have an impeccable version ready. With regards to video interviewing skills, executives seem to have a blind spot.

This book was born by the shocking mediocrity I witnessed in video based interviews with the aim to help executives close this gap. We learned the three pillars of video interviewing success to be Your Technical Choices, Your Hollywood Setting, and Your Interview Performance.

We also talked a lot about video interviewing in the context of the Hidden Job Market, which adds another layer of care and consideration. As a Morita Method Executive, you aren't sitting around waiting for the perfect job listing to be posted. No, you determine where you might fit in the executive world, and you go after it. When you find an "in" within a company, you take advantage of this human connection and use your resources to carefully insert yourself into the picture and show the "interviewer" your Unique Value Proposition.

Video interviewing is a team sport. It's all about perception and preparation. Perception is reality. That makes the video experience tricky to master on your own. Get others involved. Get their feedback on your image and video performance. Video interviewing is treacherously simple. It is all about engagement, and getting the interviewer to maintain focus on your conversation is your challenge. Executives too often take the attention window for granted, allowing the interviewer to drift into distractions. Engagement eats attention, or distraction eats attention.

Everybody can be masterful at video interviewing when you treat it as an art. It is my fondest hope that you regularly review and improve your video interviewing skills so that you will rise and shine in the next real executive-level interview to win $250K to $1M jobs with technical brilliance and authenticity.

REFERENCES

Alexander Mann Solutions (2020). "Transforming Talent Acquisition for the Future." *Aptitude Research*, https://www.aptituderesearch.com/wp-content/uploads/2020/10/Transforming-TA-for-the-Future_US_Final.pdf.

Capermint Team. (2021). "Top 26 Free Video Chat and Calling Apps in 2022." Capermint, https://www.capermint.com/blog/top-26-free-video-chat-apps/.

Gartner, Inc. (2020). "Three Approaches to Effectively Manage Virtual Interviews." Gartner, https://www.gartner.com/en/documents/3992422.

HireVue Team. (2021). "2021 year in review: Hiring trends, industry spikes and what's to come." HireVue, https://www.hirevue.com/blog/hiring/2021-year-in-review-hiring-trends-industry-spikes-and-whats-to-come.

Foss, Jenny. (2020). "How to Make Sure You Sound Like a Person (Not a Robot) in an Interview." The Muse, https://www.themuse.com/advice/how-to-make-sure-you-sound-like-a-person-not-a-robot-in-an-interview.

Love, Adam. (2020). "The World's Not on Pause! 86% of Organizations are Using Virtual Hiring During COVID-19." HireVue, https://www.hirevue.com/blog/hiring/the-worlds-not-on-pause.

Lu, Marcus. (2020). "50 Cognitive Biases in the Modern World." Visual Capitalist, https://www.visualcapitalist.com/50-cognitive-biases-in-the-modern-world/.

Mehrabian, Albert. (2009). ""Silent Messages" – A Wealth of Information

About Nonverbal Communication (Body Language)". *Personality & Emotion Tests & Software: Psychological Books & Articles of Popular Interest*. Los Angeles, self-published.

Morita, Rainer Maria. (2018). *Executive Job Search in the Hidden Job Market – The Morita Method*, CreateSpace Publishing, California, United States.

Morita, Rainer Maria. (2018). *Peak Performance Interviewing for Executives*. CreateSpace Publishing, California, United States.

Morita, Rainer Maria. (2022). *Perfect Pitching for Executives in the Hidden Job Market*. Independently published.

Morita, Rainer Maria. (2020). *Find Your Career Passion: Towards Abundant Joy, Fulfillment and Authenticity in Your Job, Career, and Life*. Independently published.

Team Kapost. (2013). "How to Prepare an Awesome Video Shoot." Upland, https://uplandsoftware.com/kapost/resources/blog/how-to-prepare-an-awesome-video-shoot/.

The University of Texas Permian Basin. (2022). "How Much of Communication Is Verbal?" https://online.utpb.edu/about-us/articles/communication/how-much-of-communication-is-nonverbal/.

Zelensky, Volodomyr. (2022). *Speech to the Russian People* [Video]. YouTube. https://www.youtube.com/watch?v=Fwzb_JX7u04

NO AUDIO SHEETS

I CANNOT
HEAR YOU ▽
o

REBOOT
ZOOM

CALL ME AT

+41 76 538 89 89

CHECK YOUR MICROPHONE

SEND ME
MS TEAMS LINK
VIA EMAIL

Rainer Maria Morita is an International Hidden Job Market Expert helping executives in Switzerland and worldwide find their perfect job based on his own job search methodology called the "Morita Method". As an Executive Job Interview Coach, he is helping CEOs and CxOs win the executive interview challenge.

Each year, more than 1,000 executives profit from his expertise. Rainer Maria partners with top-tier executives and executive contenders worldwide to help them get an edge in this ever-changing international economy. He regularly coaches alumni from INSEAD and IMD. The largest outplacement company worldwide retains him as Hidden Job Market subject-matter expert covering Switzerland, Europe and Asia.

Rainer Maria is affiliated with Lausanne-based 50-strong consultancy Excelerate Partners. Rainer Maria is also an Executive Career Advisor with Blue-Steps, headquartered in New York, which is the exclusive executive career service provider of the Association of Executive Search Consultants (AESC). AESC is the voice of excellence for the executive search and leadership consulting profession worldwide.

Rainer Maria is an international bestseller author who has published 7 books, notably *Executive Job Search in the Hidden Job Market – The Morita Method*, *Peak Performance Interviewing for Executives*, and *Perfect Pitching for Executives in the Hidden Job Market*.

With a Masters in Strategic Technology and Innovation Management from the University of Manchester, UK, and Bocconi, Milan, combined with "AI Leadership" executive education at MIT, Boston, he is uniquely qualified to help leaders define how to best win interviews so that they get the executive career opportunity they deserve and love.